Hope
in the
Struggle

Finding hope in the darkest times
90 Days
of Encouragement

Layla Freeman

Light of Hope
Publishing

About the Cover

The tree of life. As a tree grows and develops, its roots dig deeper into the earth, establishing a firm foundation. Sometimes, the environment causes disturbances and difficulties hindering the proper growth of the tree. The structure of the tree is challenged and pressured into a different direction. As the tree struggles against the environment, its shape becomes evident that it has taken on life with a hearty boldness...empowered and surviving...despite its obstacles. As I look at this particular tree, I am reminded of the ability to survive and overcome. I see the hope this tree represents. No matter how difficult, how dark, how dry, or how barren this tree was at one time, it now stands firm with a healthy terrain surrounding it. The bent angle of the trunk reveals where there was difficulty. The challenges it faced did not cause the tree to break and collapse. Instead, it overcame and survived. To me, this tree represents hope in the struggle.

ISBN-10: 0692322310
ISBN-13: 978-0692322314

Dedicated to
Randall, Savannah & Tessa:
You light up my life.

In Memory of:
My precious daughter Ashley Morgan
&
My loving Aunt Carolyn McIntosh

Special thanks to:
Carol Round, for her love, guidance, help and
encouragement, which made this book possible.

Foreword

Layla Freeman has indeed helped many people find hope in the midst of struggle. I have often found her articles in "Layla's Light" to be the spiritual lift I needed for the moment. Her willingness to authentically share from her own experience is so helpful in reminding us that we are not alone when we face the trials of life. She has faced her own struggles with an inspiring faith and determination. Through it all she has encountered the powerful grace of God. That grace is evident in her words and in the encouragement she shares throughout this book.

Dr. Ray Crawford,
Pastor, Claremore First United Methodist Church

Introduction

As I pray each morning and write the words God places in my heart, I take a chance. I recognize that everyone has an opinion, a thought or a voice to speak in response to what I might say. I do not claim to be anything other than a woman who loves God with all my heart and soul....and lives to be a disciple for Jesus Christ.

I am a simple human being with a desire to encourage and help others in any way I can. God has placed me where I am today, and I am willingly and diligently serving Him. I am a work-in-progress, learning and growing every day. The more I reflect on this, the more it makes me smile. You see, I have suffered. I have made many mistakes. I have been lost, depressed, isolated and ashamed. It took quite a while for me to find the love of God that was waiting on me. God never gave up on me. Today I am able to look back and see the beautiful journey of my healing and growth. Isn't it amazing we all have the opportunity to be loved so equally and unconditionally?

You see, God is God of all. God created us all, everyone, absolutely EVERYWHERE! For us, it is hard to comprehend the magnitude of that number. Too many times we forget there are people in this world who have never been introduced to Jesus. People are born and raised in different areas of the world and their beliefs are formed by their culture. Having lived in different parts of the world, I know this reality first hand.

One of the most important things we need to remember as we meet people today, is we all come from different places with different standards to live by, different codes of ethics and different belief systems. We can all learn from each other. What if we approached each other with a willingness to listen to each other's story and to learn what has formed us to this point?

What if we began treating each other with genuine respect and love, casting away judgment? What if we showed each other patience, empathy and gratitude? While this may sound good in theory, it can be difficult to apply in our controversial world today. However, we can show other people the love of Jesus, which in turn, can be a seed of faith planted in their hearts. We don't have to preach. We don't have to speak our opinions boldly. We simply need to love one another.

Let's remember to see the good in other people. We are all human, created by our loving Heavenly Father. We are all given the same gift of free will, and we can all receive the redeeming love of Jesus. We all hurt and we all have struggles. The difference between two people may simply be the lack of knowledge. But, we can show people our faith by living it in love and in compassion.

"Love the Lord your God with all your heart and with all your soul and with all your mind and with all your strength. The second is this: Love your neighbor as yourself. There is no commandment greater than these"
–MARK 12:30-31.

God is with us,
Layla Freeman

Day 1 _____

Are you going through something challenging right now? Do
you feel isolated and alone? Do you feel like no one understands
or cares? Do you feel resentful or bitter because your emotions
are raging out of control? We've all been there. Whether you
are going through the fire right now or have been through it in
the past, it's a very difficult place to be. Recognize that you are
normal and you are not alone. Your battle can and will be
overcome if you allow God to step in and help. So often when
we need God the most, we tend to shut Him out. It's when you
don't feel like praying that you should pray more. It's when you
don't feel like accepting help that you need help the most. It is
when you feel like giving up....that you should give it all up to
God. We cannot possibly press through the trials alone. The
devil will use these difficult times to try to bring you down
more and attempt to turn your attention away from the power of
God. Keep in mind that this world has two spiritual
realms...darkness or light. The light always, always overpowers
the darkness. Jesus is the light. God gave us His only son Jesus
to be our helper and our deliverer through each struggle. Allow
Jesus to be your light...your source. God's amazing love, grace
and mercy can and will carry you through. God's power is in
your hands if you simply ask Him to show you the way. Don't
expect instant results; instead, give God time to turn things
around. Trusting in Him will give you power and peace to
endure the challenge and be an overcomer.

*"When Jesus spoke again to the people, He said, 'I am the light of the
world. Whoever follows me will never walk in darkness, but will have
the light of life'"—JOHN 8:12.*

*"But the Lord is faithful, and He will strengthen and protect you from
the evil one. We have confidence in the Lord that you are doing and
will continue to do the things we command. May the Lord direct your
hearts into God's love and Christ's perseverance"*
—2 THESSALONIANS 3:3-5.

_____ *Your Thoughts*

Day 2

Life is hard. No matter who you are or where you are, you will face difficulty in life. Difficulties are part of our existence. We cannot escape them. No matter how hard we try or how far we run, the problems don't go away. We all need help. So, why is it so hard to admit we need help? Why is it so hard to ask? Why do we allow ourselves to continue down the road alone? The answer to these questions is pride. Pride is our enemy. It causes more issues than just the selfish definition it holds. If we don't let go of pride and admit we are weak, we are playing God. God is our Father. Our Creator. Our existence. He is our help, our guide, our source of wisdom, direction...and our HOPE. We are human, given the free will from God to make choices in our lives. This means we have the opportunity to decide how we will handle the adversities we face. We can choose to seek God and surrender our life to Him or we can continue to walk alone. Attempting life alone leads to isolation, fear and serious depression. This is when the devil will attack your mind. Don't give the devil the opportunity to keep you down, to remain hopeless...to steal...kill...and destroy. (John 10:10) ASK GOD FOR HELP. God never leaves us. We are the ones who walk away from God. Begin now by praying to God. Simply tell God you need Him. Ask Him to help you. Then, open up your eyes....open up your heart...open up your doors...because God will bring people to help you, show you signs to follow and pour down His love and blessings upon you. Give God the trust and the time and you will see His great works in your life.

"God opposes the proud but gives grace to the humble. Humble yourselves, therefore, under God's mighty Hand, that He may lift you up in due time. Cast all your anxiety on Him because He cares for you. Be self-controlled and alert. Your enemy the devil prowls around like a roaring lion looking for someone to devour. Resist him, standing firm in the faith, because you know that your brothers throughout the world are undergoing the same kind of sufferings. And the God of all grace, who called you to His eternal glory in Christ, after you have suffered a little while, will Himself restore you and make you strong, firm and steadfast. To Him be the power forever and ever. Amen"
—1 PETER 5:5-11.

_____ *Your Thoughts*

Day 3

Discouragement. Sadness. Depression. All are emotions we experience at some point in our lives. Many times we feel these emotions internally but outwardly we pretend we are just fine. These kinds of emotions can be exhausting but they are real. They are necessary at times in our lives. If we did not experience these difficult emotions, we wouldn't understand the opposite emotions of joy, happiness and peace. It is important to recognize and acknowledge your feelings of sadness, discouragement and depression. Something significant has happened to cause these feelings. In order to overcome these hard times, we must face the significant circumstances that led to these emotions. It is healthy to admit your weaknesses. It is healthy to express your heart-felt struggle. It is critical to release the pain of what you are trying to bury. Don't hold the emotions in; instead, allow them to process through you so they can be faced and dealt with. If we bottle up the real struggle, we continue to allow the pain to fester. This is when the devil finds you weak and will begin to attack you in subtle ways. It is vital to seek God at these difficult times. While you may feel isolated from God and the world, God is right there waiting to guide you and help you. Ask Him to help you battle your sadness. Ask Him to show you who to go to...where to go...and what to do. God will never fail you if you give Him the opportunity. There is a way out of this dark time of hidden emotions. All it takes is your small whisper in prayer to God. God's comfort will slowly begin to carry you through, lift you up and deliver you out of the darkness.

"Praise be to the God and Father of our Lord Jesus Christ, the Father of compassion and the God of all comfort, who comforts us in all our troubles, so that we can comfort those in any trouble with the comfort we ourselves have received from God"—2 CORINTHIANS 1:3.

"In addition to all this, take up the shield of faith, with which you can extinguish all the flaming arrows of the evil one"— EPHESIANS 6:16.

_____ *Your Thoughts*

*Day 4*_____

Sometimes you're going along in life when you suddenly hit a road block. More than one obstacle is thrown in your way, leaving you feeling as if you have done something wrong. It's a discouragement we all go through. This is the way of life...of our human nature. Challenges and obstacles are not to be looked at as if we had something to do with them...as some sort of punishment. They are simply the reality of the world we live in. Remember: the devil uses all sorts of trickery to make us get off track. Keep your mind focused on doing the right thing, regardless of your feelings. Road blocks are how we become better people. It's through adversity that we develop a strong spirit. The choice to turn to God for help in these times is the determining factor. If we seek God in our time of discouragement, then we know we will never be alone. Allow God to guide you in handling things. Soon, that discouragement will become spiritual muscle and a stronger foundation for you to be a witness.

"So do not fear, for I am with you; do not be dismayed, for I am your God. I will strengthen you and help you; I will uphold you with My righteous right hand"—ISAIAH 41:10.

"So we fix our eyes not on what is seen, but on what is unseen. For what is seen is temporary, but what is unseen is eternal"—2 CORINTHIANS 4:18.

Do not be anxious about anything, but in everything, by prayer and petition, with thanksgiving, present your requests to God. And the peace of God, which transcends all understanding, will guard your hearts and your minds in Christ Jesus"—PHILIPPIANS 4:6-7.

_____ *Your Thoughts*

_____

_____

_____

_____

_____

_____

_____

_____

_____

_____

_____

_____

_____

_____

_____

_____

_____

Day 5 _____

Oh how this world hurts. There is pain and heartache everywhere. The media highlights the tragic, horrific, astounding and mind-boggling negative things happening all around us. We are bombarded with the sin surrounding us. We can look at the crowd and see the sadness and hurt in other people's eyes. The reality is we can look in the mirror and see sadness in our own eyes. This world hurts. This world is hard to live in and a challenge to us every single day. So, given all this reality we face each day, how are we going to handle it? We can crumble when we see the negative influences in the world or we can stand up and embrace the good in this world. We don't have to hurt alone; in fact, we can overcome those hurts and cast off the sadness. We can overcome the evil and sin that can easily ensnare us. We can choose to receive Jesus as our Lord and Savior and begin allowing the love of Jesus to live within us. We can begin seeking God...our Father...to help us climb out of the pit. We can be honest and surrender our burdens and our deepest secrets to God. God forgives. God heals. God helps and does not hold grudges. God is the beginning of freedom...the deliverer...the answer to our every need. We are the ones who can make this world a better place. We are the ones who can choose to let God help us. It's up to us to allow God in. Don't let the world be the doorkeeper to your heart and your life. Make the choice today to allow Jesus to guard your heart and God to guide your life.

"Better is one day in your courts than a thousand elsewhere; I would rather be a doorkeeper in the house of my God than dwell in the tents of the wicked. For the Lord God is a sun and shield; the Lord bestows favor and honor; no good thing does He withhold from those whose walk is blameless"—PSALM 84:10-11.

"When Jesus spoke again to the people, He said, "I am the light of the world. Whoever follows me will never walk in darkness, but will have the light of life"—JOHN 8:12.

_____ *Your Thoughts*

_____

_____

_____

_____

_____

_____

_____

_____

_____

_____

_____

_____

_____

_____

_____

Day 6

Every day each one of us struggles with something. Whether it is job schedules, weight issues, depression, relationships, addiction, financial problems or the loss of a loved one, it can be a struggle to face the reality of life sometimes. God did not design us to live life alone. So why do we feel alone in our struggles at times? Losing my daughter on Christmas Eve was an extreme struggle for me. I felt alone with my grief. However, I know even with something as major as her loss, I cannot face it alone. We have a choice to seek help in our struggles and to have a partner by our side at all times. When we turn our hearts and our eyes to Jesus and ask for help, we will find the hope we need to press through. Trust in the fact that God is with you at all times. He sent His Son to help you. He gave us the Holy Spirit to guide us and give us the discernment necessary to press our way through the tough stuff. It is our job...our responsibility...to ASK for help. Once we ask we must trust that God will help us through. Soon we will look back and say, "Wow....I did it!"

"Do not be anxious about anything, but in everything, by prayer and petition, with thanksgiving, present your requests to God. And the peace of God, which transcends all understanding, will guard your hearts and minds in Christ Jesus"—PHILIPPIANS 4:6-7.

"Consider it pure joy, my brothers, whenever you face trials of many kinds, because you know that the testing of your faith develops perseverance. Perseverance must finish its work so that you may be mature and complete, not lacking anything. If any of you lacks wisdom, he should ask God, who gives generously to all without finding fault, and it will be given to him. But when he asks, he must believe and not doubt, because he who doubts is like a wave of the sea, blown and tossed by the wind"— JAMES 1:2-6.

_____ *Your Thoughts*

Day 7

Mistakes and regrets. Can you relate to those words? We all have something that makes us cringe when we recall our past. We were born, given the breath of life and the ability to make choices. We had parents or caregivers to take care of us as we grew up. We make it to adulthood and can choose our life direction. It's not easy to navigate our adult lives if we don't have a foundation in Christ. Many adults come to know Christ after having lived a pattern of mistakes and regrets. This is reality. Even those who were raised with Christ in their home have made their share of wrong choices. We're all human, coming from different walks of life, placing one foot in front of the other. So why is it so hard to admit we've made mistakes? Why do we try to cover up those past regrets? SHAME. Shame is the enemy in our subconscious. Shame is that small voice in our head whispering "You are not worthy." Shame is the devil's way of pulling you down. Holding in our guilt from what we have done in the past is like pouring fuel on burning embers. Just as soon as the embers are about to go out, they're re-ignited by the shame spewing out of our minds. YOU ARE WORTHY. YOU ARE VALUABLE. You can be forgiven for any and all things you have EVER done in your life. Jesus Christ died for us, carrying all our sins to the cross (past, present and future) so we could receive the free gift of repentance and forgiveness. God did that for you and for me. God knew we would make mistakes so He made a way for us to be free from our sins. God loves you unconditionally. Receive the love of Jesus. Believe and confess that Jesus is Lord. Then, ask God to forgive you for anything from your past. Allow your shame to be lifted away. Save yourself from unnecessary pain. You deserve this.

"That if you confess with your mouth, 'Jesus is Lord,' and believe in your heart that God raised Him from the dead, you will be saved. For it is with your heart that you believe and are justified, and it is with your mouth that you confess and are saved. As the Scripture says, 'Anyone who trusts in Him will never be put to shame.' For there is no difference between Jew and Gentile – the same Lord is Lord of all and richly blesses all who call on Him, for, 'Everyone who calls on the name of the Lord will be saved'"— ROMANS 10:9-13.

_____ *Your Thoughts*

Day 8

Where did we go wrong? Why am I being punished? How can this be happening? Why me? These are questions from the heart that we've all experienced at some time in our lives. When we face adversity, we immediately begin trying to find the reason which typically leads to pointing the finger at someone or something else. More often than not, God is the first one we blame. It's human response to wonder why our Creator...our Father in Heaven would be allowing these difficult things to happen. It makes no sense to us. We have a need to fix things and if we can figure out why things happened in the first place, we can begin to analyze how to fix it. How many of us have gone through this cycle in our lives...over and over again? Since creation humans have been struggling with this cycle of faith. Faith is not easy. Faith is something we develop. Faith is hope. Hope is what we must hold onto in order to press through the difficult times and to understand that these times are temporary. We cannot possibly understand the depths of what happens to us in our lives. The one thing we can control is our reaction to life. It's the action we take that will determine our own inner peace. The situation may not change immediately but if we can learn to seek God and open up our heart to trust Him, we can begin a new walk of faith. The more we allow ourselves to understand that God is the One who will help us, the more we grow in strength. God is the One who has the ultimate power and control. God will help...God is there...we just need to break down our walls and let Him in.

"So do not throw away your confidence; it will be richly rewarded. You need to persevere so that when you have done the will of God, you will receive what He has promised"—HEBREWS 10:35-36.

"Now faith is being sure of what we hope for and certain of what we do not see"— HEBREWS 11:1.

_____ *Your Thoughts*

_____

_____

_____

_____

_____

_____

_____

_____

_____

_____

_____

_____

_____

_____

Day 9

Someone...please hold my hand and help me get through this. Anyone...tell me I'm not alone. Friend...please tell me it's going to be okay. Jesus...help me. God...I don't know what to do. I need to know you are there. No matter who you are or where you are in life, you have experienced these emotions at some point. More often than not, we feel them repeatedly. We face difficulties and circumstances that are overwhelming. How can we possibly know how to handle some things in life when we have had no experience with the situation? We can't expect to know what to do all the time. It's not possible to be that wise. So, what do we do when we feel lost and overwhelmed? How do we make ourselves press forward when all we really feel like doing is giving up? Pray. Even if you feel as if you have no prayer in you...whisper a prayer to God anyway. Mumble...scream...or even silently pray but press forth the effort to simply pray. Don't think you have to know what to say—just say what's on your heart. Let yourself release that burden—that absolute unknown and lost feeling. God knows. He is just waiting on you to ask Him for help. Praying to God is our ultimate power tool and when we seek God in prayer, we open up our hearts to God's divine intervention. God is our Father and He will take care of you—always. God is the one who can and will carry you through if you will allow Him the opportunity to do so. Don't feel alone. Don't feel as if you can't make it through. God is there and He will bring people in your life to help you and turn situations around in a way you could never imagine. It takes time and trust in God. Believe that God is really there. Pray and then hold onto Hope and God's promises.

"Be joyful in hope, patient in affliction, faithful in prayer. Share with God's people who are in need. Practice hospitality"
—ROMANS 12:12-13.

"The prayer of a righteous man is powerful and effective"
—JAMES 5:16

_____ *Your Thoughts*

_____

_____

_____

_____

_____

_____

_____

_____

_____

_____

_____

_____

_____

_____

_____

No one ever REALLY wants to face themselves. We go to extremes to ignore, hide, cover up or redirect the issues in our own life. We point the finger at others trying to take the attention off ourselves. We buy things, work too much, eat too much, drink too much and sometimes...yes...exercise too much. Anything we can do to try and avoid 'feeling' and 'facing our own self is a habit many of us fall into in our lives. Why do we do this? The world has created a false image of what the world thinks a human being should be like. It's so far from realistic, yet people fall into the trap of trying to fit into that image. We compare ourselves to what the world shows as an example and it becomes impossible to obtain. In our attempt to try and reach that worldly standard, we begin to create issues within ourselves that would otherwise not be there. Take a good look at what you are striving toward on a daily basis. Where are you focusing your priorities? Begin to eliminate things and honestly see the obvious unrealistic measures of this world. Then, take a good look at what your personal issues are and you will see they are directly correlated to those unrealistic things you have been trying to measure up to. God desires for each one of us to be happy and abundantly blessed. He will give you more than you can ever imagine if you let go of this world and grab onto Jesus. Our hope is in Jesus and our true happiness lies within the Hope that we have in Jesus. Surrender your life to Jesus and develop a relationship with Him. Jesus will fulfill all your needs and you will find healing on the inside. Soon your personal issues will become experience and wisdom to share with others. Let go of this world and embrace the Savior Jesus Christ. He will never let you down.

"For the grace of God that brings salvation has appeared to all men. It teaches us to say 'No' to ungodliness and worldly passions, and to live self-controlled, upright and Godly lives in this present age, while we wait for the blessed hope - the glorious appearing of our great God and Savior, Jesus Christ, who gave Himself for us to redeem us from all wickedness and to purify for Himself a people that are His very own, eager to do what is good. These, then, are the things you should teach. Encourage and rebuke with all authority. Do not let anyone despise you"—TITUS 2:11-15.

_____ *Your Thoughts*

_____

_____

_____

_____

_____

_____

_____

_____

_____

_____

_____

_____

_____

_____

_____

Day 11

Exhaustion. Mental and physical exhaustion is something we all face frequently. There are days when it just seems like everything has piled up on our shoulders and we don't have a clue where to start. We spin circles around ourselves trying to keep up with life's demands, yet it seems as if we aren't catching up. We get less and less sleep. We either can't sleep because our mind is whirling with the thoughts of the how's, when's or why's or we don't get enough sleep because we are up late or early trying to cram it all in. We use coffee or unhealthy energy drinks to jump start our exhausted bodies. We rush through the drive through to save extra time and fail to eat healthy. Exercise gets placed at the bottom of the list because everything else becomes priority. We're financially strapped, over-extended in every area of our life and desperately need peace. If we aren't careful, we begin to fall into a pit of despair...which can lead to depression. Does this sound familiar? Yes, this is the world as we know it. We must analyze our lives and recognize what we are doing that is absolutely unnecessary. There are areas of our life that can be eliminated. There are areas of our lives that can be replaced with the true sustenance we NEED in order to find peace. JESUS is the bread of life...our sustenance. Jesus is our helper...our deliverer...our guide to calm and peace. If we make God a priority in life and follow the example of Jesus, we will be able to focus on the important in life. We can enjoy the important things because we will begin recognizing what is not important. We will learn balance and control when we walk in the way of the Lord. Take the time today to ask God to mold your life in the way it should be. When we slow down and give our time to God, God will give us time and rest.

"Then Jesus declared, 'I am the bread of life. He who comes to me will never go hungry, and he who believes in me will never be thirsty'"
–JOHN 6:35.

"Do not be anxious about anything, but in everything, by prayer and petition, with thanksgiving, present your requests to God. And the peace of God, which transcends all understanding, will guard your hearts and your minds in Christ Jesus"—PHILIPPIANS 4:6-7.

_____ *Your Thoughts*

Day 12

Why do things keep happening to me? Why does it seem like the harder I try to do good the more difficult things get? Why can't I get an answer to my situation? Why, why, why? Every one of us has had these internal battles. In fact, this cycle of life is never ending. As humans, we will experience ups and downs on a regular basis. Some things we face will be giant mountains, such as death, cancer, job loss, divorce and abuse. Other things are annoying bumps in our path, just enough to disrupt our life. Regardless of what we face, we don't like dealing with obstacles. On this journey, we often question the existence of God in the hardships. We wonder why we don't hear from God or why He doesn't intervene. We pray and pray but feel alone because we don't see evidence God is with us. Guess what? God is always, forever, and eternally with us. God does not leave us in the midst of our troubles. God is there, waiting for us to give our heart to Him. However, we doubt when faced with extreme hardships and it leads us to pray empty prayers. Doubt holds us back from allowing God to release all His power and forces in our situation. Our world is a spiritual battleground. The forces of evil are very powerful, and they can take over, attacking us daily. We must first acknowledge we will never know the future, and that when we are faced with these extreme hardships, we must allow God to fight that spiritual battle for us. God knows best. God is, and will always be, our ultimate power. God will carry us through whatever we face. This world as we see it is not our ultimate home. God has given us eternity to look forward to and we need to trust Him, knowing we have that hope. Do your best to eliminate the fear of the unknown which leads to doubt. Give your life and your situation to God wholeheartedly. Trust God in every aspect of your life and you will be able to press through everything this world throws at you.

"And we rejoice in the hope of the glory of God. Not only so, but we also rejoice in our sufferings, because we know that suffering produces perseverance; perseverance, character, and character, hope. And hope does not disappoint us, because God has poured out His love into our hearts by the Holy Spirit, whom He has given us"
—*ROMANS 5:2-5*

_____*Your Thoughts*

Day 13

What are you dwelling on? What are you worried about? How much time do you spend in premeditated thought about how to deal with a situation? Why do we do this to ourselves? We lose sleep. We don't eat right. We become irritable. We create headaches and stresses making it worse. Do you realize that all this exhaustion and effort is our own fault? We gain nothing by trying to control these situations that are ultimately out of our control. Have you ever considered how many times you've heard the statement "Give it to God?" The reality is God is the One whom we should be giving all the control. He is the One who controls the universe so He is more than capable of controlling our situation. In fact, God can take a horrible situation and turn it into something we could never imagine. God can take our lives and create peace and calm. It's up to us to decide how we will handle our lives right now. We can apply God's Word to our lives and believe what He says. If we start with simple trust in God's promises, we can rest assured that things will begin to work out for the good. Jesus said, *"Therefore do not worry about tomorrow, for tomorrow will worry about itself. Each day has enough trouble of its own."* (Matthew 6:34) Begin today by asking God to show you the way through today. Allow Him to lead you and you will have a life of balance—one day at a time.

"The Lord is righteous in all His ways and loving toward all He has made. The Lord is near to all who call on Him, to all who call on Him in truth"—PSALM 145:17-18.

"Therefore I tell you, do not worry about your life, what you will eat or drink; or about your body, what you will wear. Is not life more important than food, and the body more important than clothes? Look at the birds of the air; they do not sow or reap or store away in barns, and yet your heavenly Father feeds them. Are you not much more valuable than they? Who of you by worrying can add a single hour to his life?"—MATTHEW 6:25-27.

_____ *Your Thoughts*

Day 14_____

Have you ever faced something in life that left you feeling overwhelmed with fear? Sometimes we simply don't know how to process certain types of fear. Fear can be crippling and can hinder our future if we don't control it. One day, my precious mother came home to find her home broken into and ransacked by thieves. As we went through the process of calling the police and then filtering through and cleaning up the mess, fear continued to build in us. The initial fear of a situation can be shocking but the lingering fear of how to handle the future can be dangerous if we don't take control of it. The devil can use any of our fears as a way to break down our faith. As we experience fear in our lives, we need to remember the power of God. His abundant love and protection is greater than any obstacle we will ever face. It is important for us to look for the blessings in each situation. No matter how bad things can appear, we can find good within the trial. Focus on what God HAS done for you....and praise God in the storm. Use times of difficulty to seek God more. Thank God for His protection...His love...and His help. Then, ask God to help you let go of the fear and to fill you with the Grace of peace within. We must trust God with all our hearts. When we replace fear with trust in God, we gain the ultimate control and power over our lives through the hope and healing that God promises to give.

"So do not fear, for I am with you; do not be dismayed, for I am your God. I will strengthen you and help you; I will uphold you with my righteous right hand. For I am the Lord, your God, who takes hold of your right hand and says to you, Do not fear; I will help you"—ISAIAH 41: 10, 13.

"So we say with confidence, 'The Lord is my helper; I will not be afraid. What can man do to me?'"—HEBREWS 13:6.

_____ *Your Thoughts*

Right and Wrong. Good and Bad. Yes and No. These are basic concepts we know but aren't so basic anymore. The world has become a mass of confusion and grey areas. People refuse to live the right way; instead, they choose to live the comfortable way. Why is this happening? Why has the truth and righteous living become so disrupted? Humans have been confused forever. It's not a new issue. It's the same today as it was since the beginning of sin. The difference is that the topics have become more public and the people don't have good examples to follow. So how can we make a difference in this world? We can be that loving example that this world so desperately seeks. Everyone is looking for peace. Everyone wants help and hope in all the trials and tribulations they face. Everyone seeks ways to find the happiness we all desire. Everyone should be pointed to The Cross. Jesus is the answer to everything. Jesus suffered and died for you. Jesus carried all our sins to the cross so we could have hope. God raised Jesus from the dead and gave us the ability to have a peace-filled life on earth and eternal life in Heaven. All we have to do is believe and receive. Believe with our heart and confess with our mouth that Jesus is our Lord and Savior. Then, we can allow the abundant love and peace to pour into our spirit...heart...mind. We can experience the hope and help of God. He is always with us, no matter what is going on around us in this world. You will begin to desire the right...know the good...and proclaim 'yes' to the promises of God!

"That if you confess with your mouth, 'Jesus is Lord,' and believe in your heart that God raised Him from the dead, you will be saved. For it is with your heart that you believe and are justified, and it is with your mouth that you confess and are saved. As the Scripture says, 'Anyone who trusts in Him will never be put to shame.' For there is no difference between Jew and Gentile – the same Lord is Lord of all and richly blesses all who call on Him, for, 'Everyone who calls on the name of the Lord will be saved'"—ROMANS 10:9-13.

_____ *Your Thoughts*

_____

_____

_____

_____

_____

_____

_____

_____

_____

_____

_____

_____

_____

Day 16

There comes a point in our lives when we must examine our core beliefs. As we mature, we begin to struggle with what our inner spirit is feeling in comparison with what the world is throwing at us. Some people begin struggling with life at an early age while others don't face this until later. Regardless of when we begin to establish our belief system, at some point decisions will develop inside our mind, causing confusion and leaving us overwhelmed. I say this to stir our hearts toward analyzing our lives. Are you living with beliefs formed because of your surroundings? Are you feeling forced into traditions or morals you really don't feel comfortable with? Do you have a stirring in your soul that yearns for peace? Are you battling your faith because you haven't figured out what faith is yet? Rest assured you are not alone. It takes time and the willingness to open your heart and mind to develop your faith. Never let anyone force their opinion upon you. You are your own individual and God has given you free will to choose the paths you take in life. God does not force Himself upon you but waits with open arms. He is not a punishing God. God is love...peace...compassion...hope and the answer to all your questions. God does not keep a record of our wrongs or take score of our deeds. God loves us unconditionally and individually. It's up to us to seek God and His righteousness in our own faith walk. This takes time. There is a personal and intimate relationship you can have with God, slowly developed and strengthened as you begin to trust God and know Him. Take the time today to give God a chance. Ask God to lead you and show you how to begin a more peaceful, fulfilling life of faith in God.

"Taste and see that the Lord is good; blessed is the man who takes refuge in Him"—PSALM 34:8.

"Ask and it will be given to you; seek and you will find; knock and the door will be opened to you. For everyone who asks receives; he who seeks finds; and to him who knocks, the door will be opened"
— MATTHEW 7:7-8.

_____ *Your Thoughts*

_____

_____

_____

_____

_____

_____

_____

_____

_____

_____

_____

_____

_____

_____

_____

Day 17

How in the world are we supposed to stay balanced in such an imbalanced world? How are we supposed to filter the world's influences and protect our children as well? We cannot live in a box secluded from society. Yet, in order to avoid the negative influences, we have to eliminate them, right? There is a balance we must seek in the decisions we make. Yes, we must do the best we can to avoid those things that are obviously not in line with God's will. This means making conscious choices about what we watch on television, the type of friends we choose, where we go to spend free time and what outside influences we allow in our home, our job, our school or church. Life is about choices we make. There will always be sin in this world. If we develop a relationship with God and allow Jesus to be our guide and example, we will begin to see clearly the things we should avoid. When we walk in the light of God's truth, God will give us wisdom to handle all situations. We will naturally be surrounded by people who make alternative choices. The key is to be the example for them and show them love and respect. We have the opportunity to shine the light of Jesus in everything we do. Build your spiritual strength with God each day and you will be building a foundation for your family and for those you influence on a daily basis.

"I will instruct you and teach you in the way you should go; I will counsel you and watch over you"—PSALM 32:8.

"Watch your life and doctrine closely. Persevere in them, because if you do, you will save both yourself and your hearers"
—1 TIMOTHY 4:16.

_____ *Your Thoughts*

Day 18

You have been saved from disgrace and are unconditionally loved and forgiven by grace. Most of us don't really comprehend what that means. In fact, it is so huge that many times we cannot wrap our minds around this reality. Grace means we've been given what we do not deserve. Grace is God's love, God's open arms, God's forgiveness, God's desire for you to be released from the bondage of disgrace and sin. Grace gives hope. Sometimes we lose hope. That's where God's grace comes in. God knows we're going to make mistakes. However, He doesn't want us to stay stuck in a pit of guilt...destruction...emptiness. This is why God gave us His only Son, Jesus Christ. Jesus suffered, died and was resurrected on behalf of us—undeserving sinners. We don't deserve to be excused for our behavior. We don't deserve anything we haven't earned, right? WRONG. God gives us His grace anyway. God gives us what we do not deserve. God gives us a chance to receive His everything. We have the choice to receive God's grace or to resist it. It's about the choices we make. Choose to comprehend the greatness of this free gift of God's grace. Set aside the pride, vanity, arrogance and stubbornness that can keep you from accepting God's grace. Believe that God loves you, have faith and trust in Him. Pray, repent, seek, accept and begin to live a life of freedom, hope and peace, given by the grace of God.

"Grace and peace to you from God our Father and the Lord Jesus Christ"—1 CORINTHIANS 1:3.

"For by grace you have been saved through faith, and this is not your own doing; it is the gift of God – not the result of works, so that no one may boast. For we are what He has made us, created in Christ Jesus for good works, which God prepared beforehand to be our way of life"—EPHESIANS 2:8-10.

_____ *Your Thoughts*

_____

_____

_____

_____

_____

_____

_____

_____

_____

_____

_____

_____

_____

_____

Day 19

Do you ever wonder why some days are more difficult than other days? Sometimes you might find yourself noticing how "happy" everyone else seems to be while you are having an unusually difficult time. You might not understand why you have these emotional ups and downs and it can become very discouraging. Many times we try to place the blame on something else or even think "Where are you God?" This world is a difficult place to live. Human elements are constantly battling with spiritual elements. We don't see the spiritual battle going on but we must begin to recognize it for what it is. The next time you face one of those "off" days recognize it as a day of battle. Don't let the devil get into your head. He will try to use your emotions to alter your thinking. Remember that we have the power to control our emotions. Stop and pray. Stop and pray again. Each time you feel yourself sliding into that emotional pit, dig deep and ask God to help you fight the spiritual battle.

"For by grace you have been saved through faith, and this is not your own doing; it is the gift of God – not the result of works, so that no one may boast. For we are what He has made us, created in Christ Jesus for good works, which God prepared beforehand to be our way of life"—EPHESIANS 2:8-10.

"For our struggle is not against flesh and blood, but against the rulers, against the authorities, against the powers of this dark world and against the spiritual forces of evil in the heavenly realms. Therefore put on the full armor of God, so that when the day of evil comes, you may be able to stand your ground, and after you have done everything, to stand"—EPHESIANS 6:12-13.

_____ *Your Thoughts*

_____

_____

_____

_____

_____

_____

_____

_____

_____

_____

_____

_____

_____

_____

Day 20

We've all made mistakes. And we've all had to deal with the consequences of our mistakes and ultimately, we've learned from them. God knows our heart. He immediately forgives us for our mistakes as soon as we confess them, asking Him for forgiveness. Why then do so many people continue to carry around the guilt from their past? There is no reason to carry around unnecessary burdens when God has given us the amazing gift of forgiveness through His Son Jesus Christ. Accept His gift...fully. God forgives and forgets, and He gives us the opportunity to do the same. God loves us unconditionally. So the next time you start to wander into that pool of past regrets—stop yourself. Instead, be grateful and thank God right then for His forgiveness and for His unconditional love.

"Praise be to the God and Father of our Lord Jesus Christ! In His great mercy He has given us new birth into a living hope through the resurrection of Jesus Christ from the dead, and into an inheritance that can never perish, spoil or fade - kept in heaven for you, who through faith are shielded by God's power until the coming of salvation that is ready to be revealed in the last time"
—1 PETER 1:3-5.

"If we say that we have no sin, we deceive ourselves, and the truth is not in us. If we confess our sins, He is faithful and just to forgive us our sins and to cleanse us from all unrighteousness"—1 JOHN 1:8-9.

_____ *Your Thoughts*

_____

_____

_____

_____

_____

_____

_____

_____

_____

_____

_____

_____

_____

_____

Day 21_____

Mountains...valleys...deep endless pits. These are the cycles we go through in life. Some of us have experienced mostly mountains and valleys. However, many of us have experienced far too many of the deep endless pits. Some of us are fighting hard to find any edge to grab hold of, in an attempt to climb out of the deep, dark places. You may feel there is no escape and the darkness seems to be closing in on you. You are not alone. There will be something you go through that will leave you feeling hopeless. You will hear advice from everyone around you and nothing will seem to help. Why must we go through this cycle in life and where is God during these discouraging times? We are human. We are flesh and blood, created with free will to do and to choose as we desire. We make choices and sometimes choices or circumstances make us. In either case, God has not left the scene. God was there...God is here...and God always will be with us. I can tell you from personal experience it is not easy pressing through these hard times. It has been a difficult journey since the death of my oldest daughter. I've had to press through the cycles of deep endless sadness. I share this reality with you so you will know we all struggle. The key to pressing through the darkness is how we surrender the storm. Are you making a definitive effort to seek God's help? Or are you simply thinking God should help you? Are you setting aside prayer time and speaking to God specifically about what you need help with? God is your Father. God wants to hear from you. He desires for you to trust in Him. Give your struggle a chance by giving God the chance to help you through it. Seek God even when you don't feel like it and you will find God in the darkness. Then, He will gently hold your hand and help you find the edges to climb out.

"Ask and it will be given to you; seek and you will find; knock and the door will be opened to you. For everyone who asks receives; he who seeks finds; and to him who knocks, the door will be opened"
—MATTHEW 7:7-8.

_____ *Your Thoughts*

Day 22

Peace is something we can all achieve—no matter how difficult our life situations are. Peace comes from within your spirit. It is something freely given by God...when we ask for it. It must be something we are willing to take with the understanding that this world will not bring you any peace. Only God can do that. Pray for God to give you the grace of peace within. Pray for God to help you accept that peace regardless of your surroundings. Do not doubt the possibility or you will doubt God. When you believe God can and will take care of your life, then you can begin releasing your control. Once you open up your mind and spirit to that grace, peace will come. Embrace the freedom of that God-given peace. Then, share that peace-filled spirit with others, helping them in whatever way you can.

"For he himself is our peace, who has made the two one and has destroyed the barrier, the dividing wall of hostility, by abolishing in his flesh the law with its commandments and regulations. His purpose was to create in Himself one new man out of the two, thus making peace, and in this one body to reconcile both of them to God through the cross, by which He put to death their hostility. He came and preached peace to you who were far away and peace to those who were near. For through Him we both have access to the Father by one Spirit"—EPHESIANS 2:14-18.

"Do not be anxious about anything, but in everything, by prayer and petition, with thanksgiving, present your requests to God. And the peace of God, which transcends all understanding, will guard your hearts and your minds in Christ Jesus"—PHILIPPIANS 4:6-7.

_____*Your Thoughts*

_____

_____

_____

_____

_____

_____

_____

_____

_____

_____

_____

_____

_____

_____

Day 23

Sometimes we can't figure out why things happen to us. We may feel like we're doing all we can do to live the right way. Then, we're faced with a major event happens making us question things. These major events can be painful to press through and difficult to understand. But think back to the past and reflect on what you've already been through in your life. Some reflections will be pleasant; others will be not. Either way, whatever your life was like then, it has developed you into a different person today. It is how we handle the major events we face in life that force us to grow. Growth comes in different shapes and forms. Even if you were on the wrong track in the past, look at where you are today. If you aren't where you want to be today, then take a look up, honestly desire to make a change and ask God to help you. Then, trust in God, even when it seems difficult. Remember, hindering the consequences in our life, hinders the healing, which in turn hinders our growth. Trust God. Do not doubt. Soon you will be able to look back and see the healing and recognize your growth.

"Set your minds on things above, not on earthly things"
—COLOSSIANS 3:2.

"My brothers and sisters, whenever you face trials of any kind, consider it nothing but joy, because you know that the testing of your faith produces endurance; and let endurance have its full effect, so that you may be mature and complete, lacking in nothing. If any of you is lacking in wisdom, ask God, who gives to all generously and ungrudgingly, and it will be given you. But ask in faith, never doubting, for the one who doubts is like a wave of the sea, driven and tossed by the wind; for the doubter, being double-minded and unstable in every way, must not expect to receive anything from the Lord"
—JAMES 1:2-8.

_____ *Your Thoughts*

_____

_____

_____

_____

_____

_____

_____

_____

_____

_____

_____

_____

_____

_____

Day 24

Time. There are periods in our lives when time seems to stand still and we must be patient while waiting for God to allow things to line up. Then, there are fragments of our lives that seem to have gone by so fast they are fleeting memories. In both instances, time is extremely important. Cherish every moment of your life, whether you are seeing it fly by too fast or you are calmly waiting for God to answer something big. God's timing is always perfect. Allow God to do what He needs to do in your life and be thankful that He is able to work all things out for the good. God is in control. We must be grateful we can rely upon Him to take care of us always.

"There is a time for everything, and a season for every activity under heaven: a time to be born and a time to die, a time to plant and a time to uproot, a time to kill and a time to heal, a time to tear down and a time to build, a time to weep and a time to laugh, a time to mourn and a time to dance, a time to scatter stones and a time to gather them, a time to embrace and a time to refrain, a time to search and a time to give up, a time to keep and a time to throw away, a time to tear and a time to mend, a time to be silent and a time to speak, a time to love and a time to hate, a time for war and a time for peace"
— *ECCLESIASTES 3:1-8.*

"And we know that in all things God works for the good of those who love Him, who have been called according to His purpose"
— *ROMANS 8:28.*

_____ *Your Thoughts*

_____

_____

_____

_____

_____

_____

_____

_____

_____

_____

_____

_____

_____

_____

Day 25

At some point in our lives, we've probably all experienced waking up one day filled with an overwhelming feeling of sadness. We may immediately identify the cause of the emotion or we may not be able to pinpoint the reason for our sadness. All we know is that we hurt. We begin to question life. While it may be a temporary emotion for some, for others it's a daily struggle. Depression is sneaky and hard to identify at times. Depression is real and it's nothing to be ashamed about. We all have struggles in our lives. We all deal with difficult emotions. We all need help. Again, we ALL need help at times. Why is it so hard to admit when we are struggling? Why is it easier to wear a mask of false happiness? If we don't quit hiding the reality of life's hardships, then we can't face our need to seek, find and truly live in real happiness. Society has created an impossible reality; yet people tend to measure their lives based on this fake level of "social worldly acceptance." As you think about your own personal struggle, analyze how you are handling your issues. Are you attempting to press through life with "the world" as your guide? It's time to take off the mask and allow God to begin healing and helping you press through the hardships. Stop looking at the world as any kind of example and seek God for His guidance and example. Begin by praying to God, asking Him to open up your heart. Then, allow Him to begin His work in you. Surrender is the beginning of emotional freedom. God is the way. He will give you the peace and happiness you so desire.

"So do not fear, for I am with you; do not be dismayed, for I am your God. I will strengthen you and help you; I will uphold you with my righteous right hand"—ISAIAH 41:10.

"Blessed is the man who perseveres under trial, because when he has stood the test, he will receive the crown of life that God has promised to those who love Him"—JAMES 1:12.

_____ *Your Thoughts*

_____

_____

_____

_____

_____

_____

_____

_____

_____

_____

_____

_____

_____

_____

Day 26 _____

Do you really know how much God loves you? It is not something we typically attempt to comprehend. But right now—this day—recognize the capacity and immenseness of God's love for YOU! He loves you more than words can explain. He loves you unconditionally with such a love that no human can ever match. He desires for you to be happy in all areas of your life. He wants you to be blessed beyond measure. Most of all He wants you to accept all the love He has for you and understand that you deserve it. Understand His love will NEVER go away! Recognize how blessed you are today and allow God to love you by recognizing how great His love is through His Son Jesus!

"For God so loved the world that He gave His one and only Son, that whoever believes in Him shall not perish but have eternal life"
—JOHN 3:16.

"Dear friends, let us love one another, for love comes from God. Everyone who loves has been born of God and knows God. Whoever does not love does not know God, because God is love. This is how God showed his love among us: He sent His one and only Son into the world that we might live through Him. This is love: not that we loved God, but that he loved us and sent his Son as an atoning sacrifice for our sins. Dear friends, since God so loved us, we also ought to love one another. No one has ever seen God; but if we love one another, God lives in us and his love is made complete in us"—1 JOHN 4:7-12.

_____ *Your Thoughts*

Day 27

Growth and development occur on two levels. We have voluntary growth through the willingness to better ourselves in education, health, jobs, faith, etc. Then, there is involuntary growth—the growth that comes from being forced into handling adversity or situations in life. At the time of the difficulties, it is hard to view anything positive coming out of the situations. Many times we struggle with our faith...our emotions...even our health. We flounder through the struggle, trying to figure out the best way to handle it. The simplicity of this is we have one of two choices. We can choose to react in a manner that uses wisdom, maturity and trust in God; or we can rebel, acting out in anger and refusing to listen to the advice of anyone. Both instances involve growth and development. One is more difficult than the other and leads to an unnecessary extended struggle. Why do we often choose the difficult pathway? Why do we struggle trusting God? God has promised us He will never leave us. God promises us forgiveness...love...and direction if we seek Him and ask for His help. Life is full of challenges and each day we will face something new. Our reaction to life is what determines our future. Make the choice to handle each day with God in control. Trust God with all your heart. Ask God to direct your steps. Allow God into your heart so you can grow and create a more fulfilling and peace-filled life.

"Trust in the Lord with all your heart and lean not on your own understanding; in all your ways acknowledge Him, and He will direct your path"—PROVERBS 3:5-6.

"Come to me, all you who are weary and burdened, and I will give you rest. Take my yoke upon you and learn from me, for I am gentle and humble in heart, and you will find rest for your souls. For my yoke is easy and my burden is light"—MATTHEW 11:28-30.

_____ *Your Thoughts*

_____

_____

_____

_____

_____

_____

_____

_____

_____

_____

_____

_____

_____

_____

Day 28 _____

Being patient about something you have been praying about is not easy. Many times we become confused or discouraged because we don't know how to decipher between our own thoughts and hearing from God. It is not easy to analyze and many times we rush things by "trying" too hard to hear directly from God. When you are praying to God for advice and guidance about something in your life, make sure you step out of the way. Once you have prayed to God about the subject, you must trust God and have faith. Follow up in prayer by asking God to help you have patience each day. Ask Him to help you let go of your selfishness so that His Will can be done in your life. Ask Him to help you hear His voice and His direction. Don't expect a loud booming answer. Expect it to take time and soon a slow shift will happen. Before you know it, you will be clear on where God is directing you.

"Let the wise listen and add to their learning, and let the discerning get guidance"—PROVERBS 1:5.

"But without faith it is impossible to please Him, for he who comes to God must believe that He is, and that He is a rewarder of those who diligently seek Him"—HEBREWS 11:6.

_____ *Your Thoughts*

Day 29

DO NOT DOUBT. Most of us read those words and ignore them or say "yeah, right" inside our head. Doubt is an ugly word. Doubt is lack of trust...uncertainty...hesitating to believe. Doubt is parallel to fear. Doubt roars its ugly head and makes us unstable in whatever we are facing. Why do we doubt? We are human and we have been hurt. We use it as an invisible shield to protect us from whatever we doubt. It is normal to be cautious toward people...toward change...or major decisions in life. However, when we doubt the truth of God and the real promises He has made us, then we are hindering our future. The first step to real hope is to stop doubting that God can make your life better than you can ever imagine. Stop doubting that God is that big and recognize that God is THAT AWESOME! God created us. He created this world and He gave you free will to make choices. God does not force Himself upon us nor does He try to manipulate or control us. God loves us so much that He allows you freedom to choose whatever you desire in your life. If you doubt that freedom and love, then you are doubting the existence of God. God is real. God is love. God is hope. God is the One who can help you. Stop doubting and recognize that the Almighty God is capable of turning your life into something amazing. Believe and you will receive. Begin trusting God, even if you don't get instant results. Give God time to move those mountains. He wants the very best for you and if you are willing to stop doubting His greatness, you will begin seeing God's power at work in your life.

"Have faith in God," Jesus answered. "I tell you the truth, if anyone says to this mountain, 'Go, throw yourself into the sea,' and does not doubt in his heart but believes that what he says will happen, it will be done for him. Therefore I tell you whatever you ask for in prayer, believe that you have received it, and it will be yours. And when you stand praying, if you hold anything against anyone, forgive him, so that your Father in Heaven may forgive you your sins"
—MARK 11:22-25.

_____ *Your Thoughts*

_____

_____

_____

_____

_____

_____

_____

_____

_____

_____

_____

_____

_____

_____

Day 30 _____

There are times we feel emotions that we don't know how to process. It can be difficult to know whether we should ignore those stirred up feelings or to express them in a healthy way. God has created us to be emotional human beings in order to have the compassion, love, anger, and joy that encompasses what a human is about. Remember, that Jesus had the same emotions that we do. The key element in handling our emotions is self-control. Self-control is derived through the simple act of turning to God for help. If we stop ourselves from having that initial fleshly reaction and ask God to help us deal with what we are feeling, then we will be able to begin handling that emotion in a healthy way. It is always a priority to seek God first. No matter how we feel, seeking God in the middle of the "flesh" keeps us in line with the "calm Spirit"...the peace that God desires us to have.

"For the grace of God has appeared that offers salvation to all people. It teaches us to say 'No' to ungodliness and worldly passions, and to live self-controlled, upright and godly lives in this present age, while we wait for the blessed hope—the appearing of the glory of our great God and Savior, Jesus Christ, who gave himself for us to redeem us from all wickedness and to purify for himself a people that are his very own, eager to do what is good"—TITUS 2:11-14.

"But the wisdom that comes from Heaven is first of all pure; then peace-loving, considerate, submissive, full of mercy and good fruit, impartial and sincere. Peacemakers who sow in peace raise a harvest of righteousness"—JAMES 3:17-18.

_____ *Your Thoughts*

_____

_____

_____

_____

_____

_____

_____

_____

_____

_____

_____

_____

_____

_____

What do you want out of life? Are you discouraged because of the choices you made in the past have deterred you from the real desires of your heart? Do you feel you have no other option than to simply go through the routine of life as it is now? Did you know that God's greatest desire is to reward us with the desires of our heart? Seriously. God wants to give you the best of the best. God wants you to have that dream fulfilled...that happiness inside...that calming peace and the hope that you can do all things you want to do. Don't get mixed up with "worldly" desires. Focus on the whole-hearted life-long, realistic, important desires. A new outlook on life will help you see what is true and valuable. Look at where you are today. Analyze what can become better. This may mean recognizing a lack of nurturing what you have now. This may also mean you need to eliminate some things that are detrimental to your future. God can help you prioritize your life. God has the best in store for you when you are willing to give Him the opportunity to take your life to the next, best level. Give God the chance to mold your heart and He will begin to reveal how to recognize, restore, and build your dreams.

"Delight yourself in the Lord and He will give you the desires of your heart. Commit your way to the Lord; trust in Him and He will do this; He will make your righteousness shine like the dawn, the justice of your cause like the noonday sun"—PSALM 37:4-6.

"You will eat the fruit of your labor; blessings and prosperity will be yours"—PSALM 128:2.

_____ *Your Thoughts*

Don't be afraid to let go. We all have something in our life we know needs to change. Many times we hold onto things, situations, or even habits we know are not healthy, simply because the thought of making a change creates discomfort in our minds. It's easy to become complacent and allow things to continue on a day-to-day basis. We often think that simply going about our daily routine in the same way as usual will make that thing, situation, or habit go away in time. The reality is nothing will change until we make an effort to step forward in a new direction. You can be relieved...you can unload...you can find peace. It starts with accepting the fact that things need to change. Once you admit that to yourself, look to God and ask Him to show you what to do next. Press past the uncomfortable feelings and the fear of the unknown and start thinking about a better future. It is amazing how God reveals signs to you. God will give you thoughts and direction, and help you know that you can do anything through Christ who strengthens you.

"Do not be anxious about anything, but in everything, by prayer and petition, with thanksgiving, present your requests to God. And the peace of God, which transcends all understanding, will guard your hearts and minds in Christ Jesus"—PHILIPPIANS 4:6-7.

"I can do everything through Him who gives me strength"—PHILIPPIANS 4:13.

_____*Your Thoughts*

Day 33

Many times we face situations we don't know how to handle. We may have a very frustrated and sometimes even an angry outlook at whatever we are dealing with. This kind of emotion is usually the root of our own selfish perception. We get caught up in how we think things should be...instead of calmly...and wisely analyzing things from every angle. The next time you find yourself dealing with a difficult situation, step out of self. First of all, pray to God, asking Him to help you see things through His eyes. Then, do your best to look at things from a different perspective and reflect in a peaceful, mature frame of mind. Remind yourself that your reaction to the situation can change the direction of the future. Positive reactions will breed positive results. Sometimes the only positive reaction you may have is to be silent. Seek God for the wisdom to know how to handle the situation. Ask God to guide you in the right direction and then allow God the time to show you His way.

"And this is my prayer; that your love may abound more and more in knowledge and depth of insight, so that you may be able to discern what is best and may be pure and blameless until the day of Christ, filled with the fruit of righteousness that comes through Jesus Christ - to the glory and praise of God"—PHILIPPIANS 1:9-11.

"If any of you lacks wisdom, you should ask God, who gives generously to all without finding fault, and it will be given to you" —JAMES 1:5.

_____ *Your Thoughts*

_____

_____

_____

_____

_____

_____

_____

_____

_____

_____

_____

_____

_____

_____

Day 34

Some days, life can be so exhausting. We may look around and think, "How did things get so out of hand?" We are overwhelmed with responsibilities that have piled up and we don't know how to fix it. It may be that your life has made a turn in the wrong direction and you don't know how to redirect to make it better. We've all faced those times of despair, those times when you feel completely alone, even if other people are surrounding you. It's important to recognize this season in your life as a season most everyone has been through at least once. You can press through this. The key is to admit you cannot do it alone. Begin by praying to God for help and guidance. You may be so frustrated you don't think you have the ability to pray. Pray something—even if you don't feel like it. Tell God you want a new direction. Ask Him to place people in your path that will encourage and guide you. Seek God on a daily basis and push out any doubt lingering in your mind. If you will commit to even two minutes of prayer each morning, God will show up. He is waiting for you to allow Him to begin a transformation in your life. Trust Him...give Him time...and you will be amazed at what you will overcome!

"Hear me, LORD, my plea is just; listen to my cry. Hear my prayer—it does not rise from deceitful lips"—PSALM 17:1.

"Ask and it will be given to you; seek and you will find; knock and the door will be opened to you. For everyone who asks receives; he who seeks finds; and to him who knocks, the door will be opened"—MATTHEW 7:7-8.

_____ *Your Thoughts*

_____

_____

_____

_____

_____

_____

_____

_____

_____

_____

_____

_____

_____

_____

Day 35 _____

Relax. Let go of any attempt to live up to other people's expectations. Be who you are...embracing you...and loving yourself. None of us can ever be who someone else wants us to be. If you find yourself constantly trying to fulfill someone else's expectation of you, then you will never find peace. Seek God in all you do, avoiding the outside influences of this world and you will find yourself content and confident. Remember, Jesus is the One and only perfect person. God designed each one of us to be a unique and priceless individual. Empower yourself with the knowledge that you are unlike anyone else and make every effort possible to live your life to the fullest and to the best of your ability...just being YOU!

"For you created my inmost being; you knit me together in my mother's womb. I praise you because I am fearfully and wonderfully made; your works are wonderful, I know that full well"
—PSALM 139:13-14.

"For God did not give us a spirit of timidity, but a spirit of power, of love and of self-discipline"—2 TIMOTHY 1:7.

_____ *Your Thoughts*

Day 36 _____

You are more valuable than ANY physical thing in this world. You are stronger than ANY object...action...or word forced upon you. You are bigger than ANY obstacle placed in your path. YOU are more than you can ever imagine because you have the ultimate power and force on your side. With God as your Father...your guide...and your help, you can overcome anything. So often we forget how to surrender our life and our circumstances to the One who can take care of it all. You are a child of God and He will take care of your every need. It may take time but the help is continuous, even if you can't see it. Today, ask God to be your 'everything' so that you can be everything He created you to be.

"I have given you authority to trample on snakes and scorpions and to overcome all the power of the enemy; nothing will harm you"
—LUKE 10:19.

"No, in all these things we are more than conquerors through Him who loved us. For I am convinced that neither death nor life, neither angels nor demons, neither the present nor the future, nor any powers, neither height nor depth, nor anything else in all creation, will be able to separate us from the love of God that is in Christ Jesus our Lord"
—ROMANS 8:37-39.

_____ *Your Thoughts*

Day 37

Fear is something each one of us faces in some way throughout our lives. It's an obstacle that can hold us back from our full potential. Sometimes we recognize our fear but many times we just push away the subject we are afraid of and define it as unobtainable. Why do we do this? God says we are able to do ALL things through Christ who strengthens us. God did not say we can do some things and not others. It is our own decisions that make us press forward in our lives. If we are willing to recognize that what we are afraid of is sometimes our own insecurity and not the actual subject, then we can begin breaking down that fear. Ask God to help you press past your doubt. Ask God to give you wisdom and confidence to overcome your insecurities and strive toward the full potential you are capable of. Trust God to help you and the fear will subside. Pretty soon you will recognize how far you have come and how much God paved your way!

"But whoever listens to me will live in safety and be at ease, without fear of harm"—PROVERBS 1:33.

"So do not fear, for I am with you; do not be dismayed, for I am your God. I will strengthen you and help you; I will uphold you with my righteous right hand"—ISAIAH 41:10.

_____*Your Thoughts*

Day 38 _____

As we reflect back on our own past, one important thing to remember is how far we have come. Whether you are where you desire to be or even if you feel you have taken a step back, you are on a journey. Within each journey is a lesson and that lesson has made a difference in your life. Each day is a step forward in your life and it takes us one day closer to eternity. Today, make sure you acknowledge the past for what it is...past lessons...a past journey...and days filled with past memories. Right now is the time to focus on this moment...this day...and the future journey that you truly desire. So often we get hung up dwelling on the things we wish we could change from the past. Why do we do that? It does no good to reflect on your mistakes. The good comes from the lessons learned from your mistakes. Take what you have been through and grab hold of the lesson. Grab hold of what you know is the good part of the journey and do your best to make TODAY all that you desire it to be. God can show you amazing and wonderful things if you begin to plant roots in today's soil, grounded in trusting God to show you how.

"Come to me, all you who are weary and burdened, and I will give you rest. Take my yoke upon you and learn from me, for I am gentle and humble in heart and you will find rest for your soul. For my yoke is easy and my burden in light"—MATTHEW 11:28-30.

"Therefore, if anyone is in Christ, he is a new creation; the old has gone, the new has come"—2 CORINTHIANS 5:17.

_____ *Your Thoughts*

Day 39 _____

Be determined to stay on track. Determine to avoid any obstacle that tries to alter your faith. The devil is very tricky and it can be easy to become discouraged in your faith walk. Make sure you recognize the evil trickery for what it is—the devil's schemes. Do not give the enemy control of your life by becoming discouraged with God. That is exactly what the devil is trying to get you to do. Instead, stand up strong and rebuke the devil. Scream out loud and tell the devil to be gone! Pray to God constantly and He will answer. He is ready for you to seek His help at all times. You have the power to take control of the negative and turn it into positive. Remember, God has given us free will to choose our own destiny. Simply stated, there is Light and there is darkness. Choose to seek the power of God's Light...the love...the hope...the joy...and the peace that God is waiting to pour down on you!

"See to it brothers, that none of you has a sinful, unbelieving heart that turns away from the living God. But encourage one another daily, as long as it is called today, so that none of you may be hardened by sin's deceitfulness"—HEBREWS 3:12-13.

"This is the message we have heard from him and declare to you: God is light; in him there is no darkness at all"—1 JOHN 1:5.

_____ *Your Thoughts*

_____

_____

_____

_____

_____

_____

_____

_____

_____

_____

_____

_____

_____

_____

_____

Day 40 _____

Experiencing difficulties and pain is not easy to deal with. Many times we're afraid to express how deep our hurt is, even to our closest family members. We internalize our feelings so much that we don't realize the burden we are carrying within until we feel as if we're going to explode. We know we're supposed to release everything to God. But being able to do that is very difficult. Our emotions are very powerful and real. We may be so depleted with the situation we are dealing with that we cannot fathom what surrender means. How often are we too overwhelmed to pray? How often do we withdraw into our own world rather than reach out for help? How often do we build walls to hide the truth of what we are facing? No matter what you are going through, you are never alone. God knows your desperation. He knows your pain. He knows your exhaustion. He also knows you know how to ask Him for His help. He gave you the free will to make that choice. Simply ask. Four words. "God, please help me." Once you have acknowledged God, you have also acknowledged yourself. You have released your will which gives God the opportunity to begin helping you. It may not be easy. But with God—ALL THINGS are possible. God's promises are real.

"Do not be far from me, my God; come quickly, God, to help me"
—PSALM 71:12.

"Ask and it will be given to you; seek and you shall find; knock and the door will be opened to you. For everyone who asks receives; he who seeks finds; and to him who knocks, the door will be opened"
—MATTHEW 7:7-8.

_____ *Your Thoughts*

_____

_____

_____

_____

_____

_____

_____

_____

_____

_____

_____

_____

_____

_____

Day 41

There are times when you are treated unfairly, disrespected and sometimes hurt. Our human nature rises up within us instinctively and we want to strike back. This is an instant reaction, without thought and without wisdom or maturity. Learn to control your reaction to those situations or people that may have hurt you. The best reaction when you instantly "want to react," is no reaction at all. Stop and take the time to think rationally. This might only take a few seconds or it might require a longer period of time. In either instance, the few moments you take can make a huge difference in the ultimate outcome. Do your very best to step back and pray. Ask God to help you handle things appropriately. Ask God to take over. Your lack of reaction to some of life's situations can be the most powerful way to handle it. Learn to have control and more importantly, learn to show kindness, even if you don't feel like it!

"Finally, all of you, live in harmony with one another, be sympathetic, love as brothers, be compassionate and humble. Do not repay evil with evil or insult with insult, but with blessing, because to this you were called so that you may inherit a blessing"—1 PETER 3:8-9.

"For this very reason, make every effort to add to your faith goodness; and to goodness, knowledge; and to knowledge, self-control; and to self-control, perseverance; and to perseverance, godliness; and to godliness, mutual affection; and to mutual affection, love. For if you possess these qualities in increasing measure, they will keep you from being ineffective and unproductive in your knowledge of our Lord Jesus Christ"—2 PETER 1:5-8.

_____ *Your Thoughts*

_____

_____

_____

_____

_____

_____

_____

_____

_____

_____

_____

_____

_____

_____

Day 42

Have you been praying about something and it seems like nothing is happening? Sometimes it might even seem like things have gotten more difficult instead of better? What are the specific details of your prayer? Think about what you are asking for. So often we get caught up in asking God for something and expecting God to do the work for us. God has given us full capability to be self-motivated and productive individuals. God's desire for us is to grow and strengthen on a daily basis, fully relying upon Him in all areas of our life. So, if you are praying about something that you are fully capable of changing or doing yourself, then God does not want to hinder your growth! Think about what you are asking for in prayer. If you are asking for something that actually takes effort on YOUR part, then stop blaming God for not doing the work for you. God is always there to guide you and lead you. But God is not going to take away the lesson, the blessing or the growth that we all gain when we press through and conquer what God knows that we can do for ourselves.

"I call on you, my God, for you will answer me; turn your ear to me and hear my prayer"—PSALM 17:6.

"And God is able to make all grace abound in you, so that in all things at all times, having all that you need, you will abound in every good work"—2 CORINTHIANS 9:8.

_____*Your Thoughts*

Loss. At some point in our lives we will all face loss in our lives. Whether it is the loss of a loved one, a job, a divorce, or even a friendship, it releases emotions within us that can be difficult to handle. We're not taught how to process these deep emotions we are faced with. Yes, there are guide books, counselors and other resources available but the reality is we still feel lost. These hidden emotions can become detrimental to ourselves or those around us. Instead of facing the emotions, we tend to internalize them and attempt to 'move on' in life. This can lead to bitterness, anger, depression, eating disorders, and alcohol or substance abuse—all of which are painful to deal with. You may have become distant from God and maybe, even angry at Him, thinking He is punishing you. God loves you and is always here for you. He did not cause these things to happen to you. He is not the reason for your pain. God is the solution. God is there, always waiting for you to ask Him for help. God can heal you and show you how to handle your emotions. Take the first step toward freedom from the pain. Surrender your life...your emotions...your everything...to God. The surrender is in you. You can do this. You can do all things with God's help. God will begin opening doors, placing people in your path and giving you the ability to heal the hidden. God loves you more than you can ever imagine.

"In my distress I called to the Lord; I cried to my God for help. From His temple He heard my voice; my cry came before Him, into His ears"—PSALM 18:6.

"O Lord my God, I called to you for help and you healed me"—PSALM 30:2.

_____ *Your Thoughts*

Day 44_____

Many of us have been known to say "I hope things will get better soon." We use the word hope and don't apply its true meaning. Our faith in God is based on trusting God, knowing that He will provide and take care of what we cannot foresee. So when we say "we hope," we really need to take that seriously. Hope is real. It is promised. It is a hope we must have. If we trust in God, we KNOW that there is hope. We don't just hope that there is hope. Be confident in God concerning His promises. Hope is sure because it is based on the integrity of God's Word. We can all experience the reality of hope because God is the God of hope. His love will help us endure all things and soon we will receive His blessings.

"Guide me in your truth and teach me, for you are God my Savior, and my hope is in you all day long"—PSALM 25:5.

"Not only so, but we also rejoice in our sufferings, because we know that suffering produces perseverance; perseverance, character; and character, hope. And hope does not disappoint us, because God has poured out His love into our hearts by the Holy Spirit, whom He has given us"—ROMANS 5:3-5.

_____ *Your Thoughts*

_____

_____

_____

_____

_____

_____

_____

_____

_____

_____

_____

_____

_____

_____

_____

Day 45_____

How long does it take to drop down on your knees and seek God in prayer? It only takes a few moments of your day. Those few moments have the power to change your day. YOU have the opportunity to ASK God for help, for guidance, for forgiveness, for mercy, for peace, for blessings...for anything. So why is this something most people leave out of their typical day? Make the choice to create a new priority in your day. Even if you spend just two minutes in prayer, those two minutes have the power to change your life forever.

"Let the morning bring me word of your unfailing love, for I have put my trust in you. Show me the way I should go, for to you I entrust my life"—PSALM 143:8.

"The Lord is far from the wicked but he hears the prayer of the righteous"—PROVERBS 15:29.

"Commit to the Lord whatever you do, and your plans will succeed" —PROVERBS 16:3.

_____ *Your Thoughts*

_____

_____

_____

_____

_____

_____

_____

_____

_____

_____

_____

_____

_____

_____

Day 46 _____

How do you view the obstacles you face in your life? Are you completely overwhelmed and defeated by the challenge you might be facing or are you looking at it as an opportunity to make a change? So often, what we must face can be a blessing in disguise. The circumstance may seem impossible at the time; but remember—God makes the impossible, possible. What we cannot see is what God is doing to line things up to our advantage. He knows your heart and is waiting for you to honestly seek His help and trust. If you desire the outcome to be fruitful, regardless of the situation, then you have to stop trying to be in control of everything. As humans, we tend to mess things up more when we attempt to manipulate the situation. It may be the hardest thing you've ever done but surrender whatever it is to God and give Him control. Keep an optimistic attitude and learn to trust that God will work things out in a far better way than you can ever imagine!

"Trust in the Lord with all your heart, and lean not on your own understanding. In all your ways, acknowledge Him, and He shall direct your path"—PROVERBS 3:5-6.

"As the Scripture says, "Anyone who trusts in Him will never be put to shame'"—ROMANS 10:11.

_____ *Your Thoughts*

Day 47 _____

Do you realize just how much you are loved? You are loved unconditionally, eternally, and immeasurably! No matter how you "feel" in your darkest of times, you are abundantly loved! Take hold of this free gift you are given every second of every single day. Don't let go of the reality because the reality is you cannot let go of the love that God pours into you at all times. Jesus is love. Jesus lives within you. Let the love of Jesus fill your heart, soul, and mind. Let this love you receive constantly be poured out to others in everything you do. Simple daily acts of kindness...words of encouragement...or helping someone get through the hard times of life are the love of Jesus living through you.

"Therefore, as God's chosen people, holy and dearly loved, clothe yourselves with compassion, kindness, humility, gentleness and patience. Bear with each other and forgive one another if any of you has a grievance against someone. Forgive as the Lord forgave you. And over all these virtues put on love, which binds them all together in perfect unity"—COLOSSIANS 3:12-14.

"This is how God showed His love among us: He sent His one and only Son into the world that we might live through Him. This is love: not that we loved God, but that He loved us and sent His Son as an atoning sacrifice for our sins. Dear friends, since God so loved us, we also ought to love one another. No one has seen God; but if we love one another, God lives in us and his love is made complete in us"—1 JOHN 4:9-12.

_____ *Your Thoughts*

Day 48 _____

Where would we be without God? Have you ever been so lost, so overwhelmed or faced with something so extremely painful that you turned away from God? You blame God for what has happened and grit your teeth every time His name is mentioned? As flesh on this earth, we deal with human earthly emotions. We don't know how to handle certain periods of our lives, so we do the first human thing we know—we blame someone or something else. When we cannot logically understand what we are going through, then it has to be someone else's fault, right? The easiest one to blame is God. First of all, God understands. Even when we have turned away from Him, He loves us anyway. Even when we ignore any mention of His name, any prayer, or any part of the church—God is there. God does not expect us to understand the things that happen to us. We cannot wrap our minds around the reasons for what we go through. However, we can choose to understand that there is eternal life and we will know everything if we choose to believe in God Almighty. God will never leave you. God will provide comfort, help, healing and direction. With God we have hope. With God we have forgiveness for anything. With God we have a chance to live again, to love again and to be free from burdens and pain. With God, ALL things are possible. If you have slipped away and feel as if you have no one, remember you have God. Allow God to help you. Simply whisper a prayer to God and tell Him you need Him. You don't have to say how you feel. God already knows. Just tell God you need Him, and He will show you His unconditional love.

"For everything that was written in the past was written to teach us, so that through endurance and the encouragement of the Scriptures we might have hope"—ROMANS 15:4.

"So we say with confidence, 'The Lord is my helper; I will not be afraid. What can man do to me?'"— HEBREWS 13:6.

_____*Your Thoughts*

_____

_____

_____

_____

_____

_____

_____

_____

_____

_____

_____

_____

_____

_____

*Day 49*_____

Sometimes we find ourselves feeling discouraged...somewhat alone...and even sad. We've all been there—some of us more often than others. It's part of human nature, part of the emotions that we experience. We are never alone in these feelings. God understands and Jesus experienced these emotions first hand. The important thing to recognize is these times are when we must draw closer to God. It might be difficult to pray when we are experiencing these emotions but it is the most valuable thing we can do. No matter how we feel inside, we can drop to our knees and seek God's help. This simple act of trust and surrender opens the door for God to begin working even harder on your behalf.

"Have faith in God," Jesus answered. "Truly I tell you, if anyone says to this mountain, 'Go, throw yourself into the sea,' and does not doubt in their heart but believes that what they say will happen, it will be done for them. Therefore I tell you, whatever you ask for in prayer, believe that you have received it, and it will be yours. And when you stand praying, if you hold anything against anyone, forgive them, so your Father in heaven may forgive you your sins"—MARK 11:22 25.

"Be anxious for nothing, but in everything by prayer and supplication, with thanksgiving, let your requests be made known to God; and the peace of God, which surpasses all understanding, will guard your hearts and minds through Christ Jesus"—PHILIPPIANS 4:6-7.

_____ *Your Thoughts*

_____

_____

_____

_____

_____

_____

_____

_____

_____

_____

_____

_____

_____

*Day 50*_____

Do you ever feel like throwing your hands up and saying, "I quit?" You're being pulled in so many directions and you can't figure out how to handle everything. God's Word says "Let us therefore make every effort to do what leads to peace and to mutual edification." (ROMANS 14:19). Edification means 'spiritual, intellectual, or moral improvement.' So, when we take a look at the overwhelming stress we've created in our life, we need to recognize the root of the imbalance. Are we focusing on what brings us peace or improvement, which is the Word of God? We must consciously make an effort to place God first and foremost in our lives. When He is first and His Word is our guide, we will grow in peace and edification. Suddenly, you will find yourself saying, "I can do this!"

"For everything that was written in the past was written to teach us, so that through endurance and the encouragement of the Scriptures we might have hope. May the God who gives endurance and encourage-ment give you a spirit of unity among yourselves as you follow Christ Jesus, so that with one heart and mouth you many glorify the God and Father of our Lord Jesus Christ"—ROMANS 15:4-5.

"Let us then approach God's throne of grace with confidence, so that we may receive mercy and find grace to help us in our time of need" —HEBREWS 4:16.

_____ *Your Thoughts*

_____

_____

_____

_____

_____

_____

_____

_____

_____

_____

_____

_____

_____

Most of us can honestly say that there have been times in our lives we have called out to God asking, "God, where are you?" We have felt abandoned...afraid...and lost. We've experienced an array of confusing emotions. This is human and this is where we must dig in and TRUST God. Every one of us has been through impossible situations, not knowing how we could possibly get through it; however, in the end, we can look back and clearly see how God brought us through it. So many times we forget these past situations...these past proofs of God's extraordinary love and power in our lives. So, if you begin experiencing the human emotions of doubt, fear and confusion, seek the Word. Drop down to your knees in prayer and tell God how you are feeling. He understands your human emotions. His Son, Jesus, is our example. He is constantly working and aligning things to help you—things we cannot visibly see. God can only work on your behalf if you ask Him to. God is ready and waiting to do ALL things, seemingly impossible things, but we must seek Him...reach out for Him...and find Him on our own.

"The God who made the world and everything in it is the Lord of heaven and earth and does not live in temples built by hands. And He is not served by human hands, as if He needed anything, because He Himself gives all men life and breath and everything else. From one man He made every nation of men that they should inhabit the whole earth; and He determined the times set for them and the exact places where they should live. God did this so that men would seek Him and perhaps reach out for Him and find Him, though He is not far from each one of us. For in Him we live and move and have our being. As some of your own poets have said, 'We are His offspring'"
—ACTS 17:24-28

_____ *Your Thoughts*

*Day 52*_____

There are two things that can rob you of your true potential. Regret for the past and fear of the future. If you dwell on past mistakes, you can release this bondage through the saving grace of Jesus. Ask for forgiveness and then truly release your past to God. At that moment, God has forgiven your past—so should you. Once you accept the free gift of that forgiveness, embrace the future as a gift of open opportunity. Trust God to lead your way and the fears you had of your future will be replaced with excitement and anticipation of what you can and will accomplish!

"Surely God is my salvation; I will trust and not be afraid. The Lord, the Lord is my strength and my song; He has become my salvation" — *ISAIAH 12:2.*

"There is no fear in love. But perfect love drives out fear, because fear has to do with punishment. The one who fears is not made perfect in love"—1 JOHN 4:18.

_____ *Your Thoughts*

Day 53 _____

So often we concern ourselves with what we will say or do when faced with different situations in life. We fret and wonder, speculating on the unknown and many times develop stress over nothing. The emotions that go along with handling life can be overwhelming. When we feel as if we simply don't know what to do, we may allow fear to creep in. Fear can be crippling and can lead you to erect walls around yourself. These walls hinder your abilities and many times you may be missing the very solution God is trying to lead you to. The best thing to do at these times is to PRAY and ask for the Holy Spirit to give you the words to speak and the actions to take. Then, stop creating scenarios in your head and begin to trust the Holy Spirit who is sent by God. He will show you exactly what to do!

"When you are brought before synagogues, rulers, and authorities, do not worry about how you will defend yourselves or what you will say, for the Holy Spirit will teach you at that time what you should say" — *LUKE 12:11-12.*

"For he has rescued us from the dominion of darkness and brought us into the kingdom of the Son he loves, in whom we have redemption, the forgiveness of sins"—COLOSSIANS 1:13-14.

_____ *Your Thoughts*

Day 54

There are days when it seems hard to take a step forward. Life can be so overwhelming...so full...and so exhausting. We can be left feeling so depleted that it's even difficult to think of what to say in prayer. Our Spirit knows we need to pray but our worn-out body can't seem to put the thoughts together. It is at these times we must not give up on prayer. We must give in to the Holy Spirit. The act of simply saying, "I do not know what to pray" is enough. The Holy Spirit helps us in our weakness. God did not leave us without strength from Him. We have all we need when we trust in God and hold onto hope. Reach out to God right now and He will reveal His presence by filling you with the ability to press past the fear and move forward in a new direction.

"When you are brought before synagogues, rulers and authorities, do not worry about how you will defend yourselves or what you will say, for the Holy Spirit will teach you at that time what you should say" —*LUKE 12:11-12.*

"But if we hope for what we do not yet have, we wait for it patiently. In the same way, the Spirit helps us in our weakness. We do not know what we ought to pray for, but the Spirit Himself intercedes for us with groans that words cannot express"—ROMANS 8:25-26.

_____ *Your Thoughts*

Some days are just hard. Why is that? We've all had days where we've felt as if things were just "off" all day long. Sometimes, these days overlap and before you know it, we're battling depression and feeling isolated. At these times in our lives, we may feel like we are all alone and that no one else understands. The truth is everyone has experienced a low point in their life and everyone has felt alone. It's so important to reach out for help beginning with asking for God to intervene. The devil loves to feed our mind at these difficult points in our lives. Satan creeps in, attempting to attack when he knows you are struggling. We must recognize that no matter how we feel, God is with you. Call on the name of Jesus and put on your spiritual fighting gloves. When we begin to understand the battle we're facing internally is a spiritual battle, we can begin to overcome the enemy. Jesus has given each of us authority to overcome the enemy and overcome any obstacle we may face in this world. Claim that victory believing that God's power is greater than anything. Press into that truth and continue praying. God will restore you and revive you and you will look back one day and recognize Jesus carried you through.

"Jesus said, 'I have given you authority to trample on snakes and scorpions and to overcome all the power of the enemy; nothing will harm you'"—LUKE 10:19.

"Finally, be strong in the Lord and in His mighty power. Put on the full armor of God so that you can take your stand against the devil's schemes. For our struggle is not against flesh and blood, but against the rulers, against the authorities, against the powers of this dark world and against the spiritual forces of evil in the heavenly realms. Therefore, put on the full armor of God, so that when the day of evil comes. You may be able to stand your ground, and after you have done everything, to stand"—EPHESIANS 6:10-13.

_____ *Your Thoughts*

_____

_____

_____

_____

_____

_____

_____

_____

_____

_____

_____

_____

_____

_____

Are you able to start a car without turning the key or pushing a button? Are you able to walk without placing one foot in front of the other? Are you able to do much of anything without first performing some sort of action to make something happen? I ask these questions to help us understand that we have to be pro-active in order to see change. So often people get frustrated in life because things aren't happening like they are praying they will. Praying about something is the first step. The second step is using the common sense and resources God provides to begin moving forward. Often people pray and then expect an instantaneous miracle. God answers prayers. That is a promise. However, God gives us opportunities to take action toward those prayer requests. God gives us people and places and opens doors that would not have come along if we had not prayed for help. Recognize that we must be willing to grab hold of what God places in our path. Sometimes, what we are asking for is not the best thing for us. God will reveal something even better if we trust Him. Open your heart to see or hear God's direction. Don't expect a loud voice from the Heavens booming down a clear message. God's guidance is subtle. Continue praying about your situation and be ready to step forward when you feel that nudging. Allow Jesus to take your hand and trust in God's timing. He knows what's best for each of us.

"Trust in the Lord with all your heart and lean not on your own understanding. In all your ways acknowledge Him, and He shall direct your path"—PROVERBS 3:5-6.

"Devote yourselves to prayer, being watchful and thankful"
—COLOSSIANS 4:2.

"Therefore, prepare your mind for action; be self-controlled; set your hope fully on the grace to be given to you when Jesus Christ is revealed"—1 PETER 1:13.

_____ *Your Thoughts*

We've all been hurt at some time in our life. As you reflect back on a past hurt, can you see your growth since that time? Have you taken that experience and learned from it, or have you buried it deep inside, allowing bitter roots to grow? The experiences we have been through mold us into what we are in the future. The pain may have been severe, but that pain doesn't need to stick with you as if you were suffering from a chronic disease. We have the choice to heal. We have the choice to take what we have gone through and make something good come out of it. I had to learn this the hard way. I suffered through twelve years of severe abuse. It took me years to escape and even more years to figure out I was still suffering from the abuse, even though I was in a safe environment. Healing is a process and it is a mindset you have to choose. God can and will heal you from your pain and suffering. First, we must understand we have to seek God sincerely, asking Him to help you begin releasing the bitter roots. Ask Jesus to take your hand and walk you through the steps of surrender. Surrendering the past means dropping to your knees in prayer and giving each one of your painful experiences to God. Picture yourself handing Jesus each emotion and each memory. Then, imagine yourself being held closely and comforted by our Heavenly Father. This act of surrender will help you to begin releasing the burdens you do not need to carry. As healing takes place, wisdom becomes your friend. Soon, you will realize you are an overcomer and the things you have been through will give you strength and courage to continue on and help someone else along the way.

"The Lord is righteous in all His ways and loving toward all He has made. The Lord is near to all who call on Him, to all who call on Him in truth"—PSALM 145:17-18.

"He heals the brokenhearted and binds up their wounds"
—PSALM 147:3.

"You, dear children, are from God and have overcome them, because the one who is in you is greater than the one who is in the world"
—1 JOHN 4:4.

_____ *Your Thoughts*

Day 58

Prayer is power. Prayer is effective. Prayer is one of the simplest things we can do to make a huge difference in our lives. Then, why is prayer so hard sometimes? I can remember times when I didn't know how to pray. I would sit down and think, but I had no idea what I was supposed to say to God. I spent years repeating the same prayer. I heard people talk of intimate prayer time with God, but I didn't get it. Finally, one day, in one of my darkest hours, I began crying out to God. I poured out my heart. I told Him what I felt...what I needed...and asked Him why? Yes, why? I felt something happen in my heart that I had never felt before. I had a sense of knowing. I knew God had heard me. I knew God understood my words...my emotions...and my doubt. It was okay to question Him. It was okay to plead and cry to Him. It was amazing to know I could actually speak to God in such a personal way. I began to understand what prayer was all about. Prayer is not something that we 'get right' or 'wrong.' Prayer is communication with God. Prayer is personal. Prayer is your time to talk to God about you, your family, your health or someone else or situations— anything. God did not give us a manuscript to follow. God gave us a heart and a mind and free will to seek out the truth. As I have grown in my faith, I have also developed a deeper intimacy and the ability to be more specific in prayer. This comes with time. I also developed an understanding that prayer out loud with a group is simple as well. Don't be afraid to pray. The simple act of talking to God opens up the doors to your heart where God can walk in and help you.

"Jesus said: 'Therefore I tell you, whatever you ask for in prayer, believe that you have received it, and it will be yours. And when you stand praying, if you hold anything against anyone, forgive him, so that your Father in Heaven may forgive you your sins'"
—MARK 11:24-25.

"And the prayer offered in faith will make the sick person well; the Lord will raise him up. If he has sinned, he will be forgiven. Therefore confess your sins to each other and pray for each other so that you may be healed. The prayer of a righteous man is powerful and effective"—JAMES 5:15-16.

_____ *Your Thoughts*

Day 59

Do you ever look around and think, why does everyone else seem to have it all together? Most of us have felt this way at some point in our lives. When we overload our lives and we feel a sense of panic, it's time to stop...drop...and pray! It's not the fact that other people 'have it all together.' That is a false perception. The fact is other people are facing difficulties of their own. We all have 'stuff' in our life. We all go through the peaks and valleys of this world. The key to handling life is our foundation...our source of strength and wisdom...our faith. God is our rock. Jesus is our helper. When we determine to dig into our faith and trust God to guide our lives, we can begin to put our lives back together. It will take time and pruning to find the balance we all need. Structure your day so that prayer is more important than your coffee to get you started. If you will commit to seeking God on a daily basis and trust Jesus to carry you through, you will recognize a sense of fulfillment in your life—of purpose and peace.

"Commit to the Lord whatever you do, and your plans will succeed"
—PROVERBS 16:3.

"Jesus says: 'Ask and it will be given to you; seek and you will find; knock and the door will be opened to you. For everyone who asks receives; he who seeks finds; and to him who knocks, the door will be opened'"—MATTHEW 7:7-8.

_Your Thoughts

Day 60_____

What do you think of when you hear the word 'HOPE'? Is it just a word easily thrown into a sentence to emphasize our desire to want something? Often times the word 'hope' is minimized into simplistic human terms. We often hear people say things such as, "I hope that happens," or "we can only hope." Why have we lost touch with the power of what HOPE really means? Hope is an assurance. Hope is the gateway to the future. Hope is an anchor to hold onto to sustain us through trials and difficulties. Jesus Christ gave us hope. When you're at the end of your rope and you feel as if there is nowhere else to turn, you can call on the name of Jesus. Jesus is our hope and our help. Hope never fails. God has given us this promise—this gift. This precious truth is always available to you. Surrender your life to Jesus and know that no matter what you face in this world, you can make it through because we have the assurance of hope in our Savior Jesus Christ.

"Let us hold unswervingly to the hope we profess, for He who promised is faithful"—HEBREWS 10:23.

"Dear friends, now we are children of God, and what we will be has not yet been made known. But we know that when He appears, we shall be like Him, for we shall see Him as He is. Everyone who has this hope in Him purifies himself, just as He is pure"—1 JOHN 3:2-3.

_____ *Your Thoughts*

Day 61

We stand before mountains in awe of their majestic beauty. The unique qualities of the landscape take our breath away. We may look from afar and see only the outline standing boldly against the blue sky. At other times, we may have the opportunity to stand at the base looking toward an endless terrain with no possible view of the top. In either case, we all know there is a top to every mountain—a place where you have reached the highest possible point. We also know there is another side to these mountains, which has its own unique terrain—its own beautiful view. The "life" mountains we face hold the same truth. You may be facing something that seems impossible to overcome. However, the truth is there is nothing that cannot be faced...climbed...or conquered when we ask Jesus to help us overcome it. We need Jesus more than we need anything else on this earth. Jesus will help you overcome the fear of whatever mountain you are facing. Surrender your heart to the one who loves you more than you can ever imagine. Don't try to face the difficulties of life on your own. Ask Jesus to help you climb these mountains. Jesus will show you the way to the top and God will deliver you into the most beautiful new terrain on the other side.

"Your love, O Lord, reaches to the heavens, your faithfulness to the skies. Your righteousness is like the mighty mountains, your justice like the great deep. O Lord, you preserve both man and beast. How priceless is your unfailing love! Both high and low among men find refuge in the shadow of your wings. They feast on the abundance of your house, you give them drink from your river of delights. For with you is the fountain of life; in your light we see light"—PSALM 36:5-9.

"Jesus said: 'I tell you the truth, if you have faith as small as mustard seed, you can say to this mountain, 'Move from here to there' and it will move. Nothing will be impossible for you'"—MATTHEW 17:20.

_____ *Your Thoughts*

_____

_____

_____

_____

_____

_____

_____

_____

_____

_____

_____

_____

Day 62

There is healing power in forgiveness. Most of us have been hurt at some point in our lives, leaving us harboring resentment toward someone. Those experiences can be dangerous to our spirit if we allow them. We might not realize what is happening within, until we suddenly become aware of how much that internalized UN-forgiveness has festered into bitterness, rage, hate or anger. These emotions are detrimental to our mental health because they don't impact the person who hurt you; they only damage your inner spirit. Even if someone has hurt you more than words can express, you must learn to release those dangerous unhealthy feelings. God asks us to forgive one another just as He has forgiven us. God does not ask us to do this because it's a command. God asks us to forgive because forgiveness is power and healing. When we forgive, we release the responsibility of holding onto the negative. Forgiving someone does not mean we forget what has happened; it means we no longer dwell on the pain. Instead, we begin to seek healing. As we make a choice to forgive, we make a second choice to hand the issue over to God. Pray for the person who hurt you. Pray for God to heal them. Pray for God to help you release the negative emotions and for you to begin healing and finding peace. This is where you find power. When you make the decision to forgive, you gain a sense of control over your well-being. You no longer allow those negative emotions to control you. Give God the opportunity to restore peace to your life and bring healing to all those involved.

"Get rid of all bitterness, rage and anger, brawling and slander, along with every form of malice. Be kind and compassionate to one another, forgiving each other, just as in Christ God forgave you"
— *EPHESIANS 4:31-3.*

"Therefore, as God's chosen people, holy and dearly loved, clothe yourselves with compassion, kindness, humility, gentleness and patience. Bear with each other and forgive whatever grievances you may have against one another. Forgive as the Lord forgave you. And over all these virtues put on love, which binds them all together in perfect unity"—COLOSSIANS 3:12-14.

~123~

_____ *Your Thoughts*

Day 63_____

Always remember who is in control. The absolute ultimate power and control in our lives is not us...or the world...or anything in it. God is everything, who created everything, and is in control of everything. Do not worry about what the future will hold. YOU MUST TRUST AND SURRENDER TO GOD. It is when we doubt the magnitude of God's power that our lives lose control. If we place God first and foremost in our hearts, minds, and spirit, we will always be okay. Remember this world and everything in it is temporary. Jesus shared our human struggles in this world. He understands what we face and He provided hope and an eternal goal for us through His death and resurrection. Seek Jesus for help and comfort. Pray to God for guidance daily. Focus on eternity and let God be in control of your future. He will take care of you.

"Trust in the Lord with all your heart and lean not on your own understanding. In all your ways acknowledge Him, and He shall direct your path"—PROVERBS 3:5-6.

"But seek first His kingdom and His righteousness, and all these things will be given to you as well. Therefore do not worry about tomorrow, for tomorrow will worry about itself. Each day has enough trouble of its own"—MATTHEW 6:33-34.

_____ *Your Thoughts*

Day 64

Help me. Two words that are powerful and life changing filled with hope. Why is it so hard to admit or say these two words? How often have we done everything we can to ignore the need for help? We skate around the issues we are struggling with, often changing the subject as soon as we can. We hide our imperfections and we exhaust ourselves doing everything we can to avoid admitting we need help. Why? We are human and we don't like to admit fault. Why? Because the world screams a false message of "perfectionism" and pride becomes more important than healing. Pride creeps in when the world and its false reality becomes the priority in life. We must recognize that pride is our enemy and that there is no situation or circumstance too big for God. We need help. Each of us needs help with something we are struggling with but did you know God wants to help us with our struggles and needs. Take away the walls you have built up around the issues. Allow yourself to be honest about those issues. Ask God for help. Ask Jesus to help you step out of the habit of pride and rest in His secure arms. Ignore what the world says and seek God's Word. What does it say? God promises to always be there. Reach out and allow God to be there for you. Simply ask God, "Help me." The power in those two words can change your life forever.

"I sought the Lord, and He answered me; He delivered me from all my fears. Those who look to Him are radiant; their faces are never covered with shame. This poor man called, and the Lord heard him; He saved him out of all his troubles. The angel of the Lord encamps around those who hope in Him, and He delivers them. Taste and see that the Lord is good; blessed is the man who takes refuge in Him" —PSALM 34:4-8.

"So we say with confidence, 'The Lord is my helper; I will not be afraid. What can man do to me?'"—HEBREWS 13:6.

_____ *Your Thoughts*

_____

_____

_____

_____

_____

_____

_____

_____

_____

_____

_____

_____

_____

Day 65

This morning I began weeping as I prayed to God. My heart is so full of compassion for all the people and situations I have been specifically praying about. My heart and mind wants to help everyone. If there were a way I could remove the pain or heal the broken hearts or lift the burdens or give money to everyone in a financial crisis or help others overcome depression, addiction or loss of hope, I would. I know that Jesus is the source of healing and my prayers are one way I can help. I weep because Jesus died and suffered for all of us so that He could help everyone. I weep because this world so desperately needs Jesus, yet they reject or ignore Him. I weep because the way my heart yearns to help others is only a tiny spark compared to God's love for all of us. I imagine that God weeps for us when we neglect to seek Him. God yearns to help everyone. God gave the most precious gift possible—His Son Jesus—so that we would have eternal hope. Do you understand the magnitude of this free and priceless gift we have all been given? Every day I pray to be all that God asks me to be. I strive every day to make a difference, attempting to help a broken world. Jesus needs all of us to come together and allow Him to help us, to help each other. I pray that today you will pick up your cross—however broken you may feel—and do one kind thing for someone else. It doesn't take much. Simply smile...give a compliment...or lend a helping hand. This act of simple love to one another will spark and ignite your heart and you will feel that compassionate spirit flow through you, which is God's love in action.

"Let love and faithfulness never leave you; bind them around your neck, write them on the tablet of your heart"—PROVERBS 3:3.

"Praise be to God and Father of our Lord Jesus Christ, the Father of compassion and the God of all comfort, who comforts us in all our troubles, so that we can comfort those in any trouble with the comfort we ourselves have received from God"—2 CORINTHIANS 1:3-4.

_____*Your Thoughts*

Day 66

How much do you try to earn God's love and forgiveness? Unfortunately, there is a misconception in the world that sends out a message of false pre-requisites. To be a Christian, to receive Jesus Christ into your heart, and to be loved unconditionally is a free gift to anyone...anywhere...at any time. There is no test you have to pass or duty you have to perform in order to receive God's grace. Being a Christian does not mean you give up enjoying life. It means you enjoy the fruits of life that God freely gives on a more fulfilling level. There is no amount of 'works' you can do that will earn your way into God's heart. You are God's creation—His sons and daughters—that He loves eternally. As we live our lives on a daily basis, we make choices to walk with Jesus or to attempt to walk on our own. The human condition causes us to waiver at times in our lives. God loves us anyway. Grace is the ultimate gift of God's love. Even when we do not deserve it, God gives us His love, His help and His hope. As we press through the trials of our lives, let us always give thanks for God's amazing grace.

"And God is able to make all grace abound to you, so that in all things at all times, having all that you need, you will abound in every good work. As it is written: 'He has scattered abroad His gifts to the poor; His righteousness endures forever"—2 CORINTHIANS 9:8-9.

"Let us then approach the throne of grace with confidence, so that we may receive mercy and find grace to help us in our time of need"—HEBREWS 4:16.

"Grace, mercy and peace from God the Father and from Jesus Christ, the Father's Son, will be with us in truth and love"—2 JOHN 3.

_____ *Your Thoughts*

Day 67

Keeping it real. Those three words have a deep meaning. Every day we face life...real life...life that can sometimes be almost unbearable. We all live on a roller coaster, riding through each day with our ups and downs. We struggle but this world makes it difficult to be honest about them. It's become a game with the actors being everyone around us. We put on a mask, erect walls and hide our trials. We plaster on fake smiles, clothe ourselves in "just fine" platitudes and hide our reality. It's difficult to do but we manage to perform our acting roles quite well. Occasionally, we find someone we trust enough to share a small part of what we've hidden. Even then, our guards are up and we rarely disclose everything. Why do we walk around pretending this isn't happening? We should be helping others press through the difficulties. We have wisdom to share if we're willing to be honest with each other. The problem is we've all experienced the world's harsh judgment. Why do we judge each other when we face similar things in our lives? God desires for us to seek His help in all we do. He asks us to love one another and help each other, not judge one another. The reality is the person standing next to you is probably dealing with the same issues you are. Let's stop judging people and start helping people press through it. Pray for God to give you discernment about who you can begin sharing with. He will lead you toward the right people who can begin encouraging you through the difficulties. As with everything in life, it all begins with prayer and the willingness to allow God to guide your way.

"Jesus said: 'Do not judge, or you too will be judged. For in the same way you judge others, you will be judged, and with the same measure you use, it will be measured to you. Why do you look at the speck of sawdust in your brother's eye and pay no attention to the plank in your own eye? How can you say to your brother, 'Let me take the speck out of your eye,' when all the time there is a plank in your own eye?'"—MATTHEW 7:1-4.

"A new command I give you: Love one another. As I have loved you, so you must love one another. By this all men will know that you are my disciples, if you love one another"—JOHN 13:34-35.

_____ *Your Thoughts*

—————————————————————

—————————————————————

—————————————————————

—————————————————————

—————————————————————

—————————————————————

—————————————————————

—————————————————————

—————————————————————

—————————————————————

—————————————————————

—————————————————————

—————————————————————

Day 68

What do you do when you just "don't want to" anymore? We've all been there. You may be there right now. Some of us have the "I don't want to's" on a daily basis. It can be habitual thinking or it may be a moment of exasperation. We face roadblocks in our lives leaving us feeling helpless and hopeless. We take the advice of those around us and we attempt to "see the positive" and pray, pray, pray. Instead of feeling as if we're moving forward, we feel like we're facing even more. How are we supposed to go through even more when we already want to give up? Why do things happen when we're making more effort to seek God? So, what are the answers? Biblical scholars have tried to answer these questions for centuries. It's not a new subject. We can't possibly know all the answers. What we DO know is that God is not punishing us or causing things happen on purpose. God is love, and more than anything, God desires for us to be free from burdens. Many times we only seek God in a more intimate way when we are desperate for God's help. We tend to use God as a temporary fix instead of relying upon Him as our source of existence. God gave us His only Son Jesus Christ. God watched His Son suffer and die for us so we could receive help and eternal life. God knows what you're going through today. Seek His help. We must never forget that God made a way for us to press through. Surrender your heart to Jesus who is the way...the truth...and the life. Face each day with the hope we have in Christ Jesus. Build your faith by surrendering each obstacle to God in prayer, not just when you need help, but every single day. Make the effort to build a relationship with God and He will fight the fight for you, and your life will begin to shift in a new direction.

"For God so loved the world that He gave His one and only Son, that whoever believes in Him shall not perish but have eternal life. For God did not send His Son into the world to condemn the world, but to save the world through Him"—JOHN 3:16-17.

"When Jesus spoke again to the people, He said, "I am the light of the world. Whoever follows me will never walk in darkness, but will have the light of life"—JOHN 8:12.

_____ *Your Thoughts*

"Get over it." "Deal with it." "Suck it up." "Move on." "Man up." "Put it behind you." The phrases could go on and on. Where does this pressure come from? Why? We live in a world used to denying reality. People would rather give advice on how to get through the problems than give advice on how to effectively work through the problem in a healthy way. Our society standard is to live day to day outwardly appearing to be 'normal'. When life throws us a curve ball, we're expected to handle it in an expedited manner. Hurry up and figure out a solution so you can go back to being "normal" again. This ridiculous cycle puts too much pressure on people. It has created a void in human compassion and love. People think they can't be "normal" if they are experiencing difficulties in life. The vulnerability is quickly pushed away, neatly hidden in the depths of the soul. When the hidden issues are not dealt with, they become like an open wound, never healing and growing more infectious each day. As the hidden wound begins to surface, we face the risk of revealing our abnormalities. We begin to look for ways to hide them so we won't have to face them. Addictions...eating disorders...depression and over exercising are just a few of the things we use to hide the truth. It's a difficult reality to accept, but we must begin facing the truth of these issues. It's time to stop covering up life. It's time to face our innermost issues and allow ourselves the time needed to heal. The first step to beginning this process is allowing God to take over your life. Accept Jesus into your heart and ask Jesus to be your helper. Jesus will walk you through this journey, step-by-step. God is waiting for you to seek Him and allow Him to begin healing you. Ask God to help you. Soon you will begin healing and finding the freedom of peace we all desire.

"My purpose is that they may be encouraged in heart and united in love, so that they may have the full riches of complete understanding, in order that they may know the mystery of God, namely, Christ, in whom are hidden all the treasures of wisdom and knowledge"
—COLOSSIANS 2:2-8.

_____ *Your Thoughts*

_____

_____

_____

_____

_____

_____

_____

_____

_____

_____

_____

_____

_____

_____

Day 70

It is tough to walk toward the unknown. It's not easy to lay down your concerns and surrender them to God. This is called complete trust in God and many times our human emotions make it very difficult to trust. This is when we must dig deep into the Word of God. We must follow the examples of those in the Bible—those who trusted God completely and were overwhelmingly blessed in the end. When you feel as if things are simply impossible and you realize your efforts to fix it all have not worked, recognize God's calling. God is waiting for you to give it ALL to Him. He cannot do what you don't give Him. So...give it God...really...give it to God.

"Trust in the Lord with all your heart, and lean not on your own understanding. In all your ways acknowledge Him, and He will direct your path"—PROVERBS 3:5-6.

"May the God of hope fill you with all joy and peace as you trust in him, so that you may overflow with hope by the power of the Holy Spirit"—ROMANS 15:13.

Your Thoughts

Day 71

As I was taking the last sip of my morning coffee, I saw my reflection in the bottom of the mug. My eyes were looking back at me. It hit me then that I never really look into my own eyes. I subconsciously place contact lenses or apply mascara to my eyelashes but I never really take the time to look inside. Am I doing this purposefully? I suddenly realized my answer to that question is yes. Why do I avoid looking into my own eyes? I know I avoid looking into other people's eyes at times because it can seem inappropriate or awkward. It depends on the circumstance, I guess. If it's a casual passing, the depth of what eye-to-eye communication reveals may be unnecessary. However, if I want to see the truth in someone's heart or the seriousness of their soul, I must see them eye-to-eye. As Jesus said in Matthew 6:22, "The eye is the lamp of the body. If your eyes are good, your whole body will be full of light." As I reflect on my own honesty, I recognize why I avoid looking into the depth of my own eyes. Vulnerability, insecurity, grief and the unknown are all revealed if you were to look deep into my eyes. We all have deep inner battles we often avoid facing. God doesn't want us to continue facing these battles on our own. If we do not admit them to ourselves, then we cannot truly surrender them to God. Let us all begin to look into our own eyes and release the things we know we need help with. One by one, as we seek God's help in prayer and surrender, we will begin to feel our spirit strengthen and our lives will be peaceful.

"I pray also that the eyes of your heart may be enlightened in order that you may know the hope to which He has called you, the riches of His glorious inheritance in the saints, and His incomparably great power for us who believe. That power is like the working of His mighty strength, which He exerted in Christ when He raised him from the dead and seated him at His right hand in the heavenly realms, far above all rule and authority, power and dominion, and every title that can be given, not only in the present age but also in the one to come"—EPHESIANS 1:18-21.

_____ *Your Thoughts*

Day 72

Do you really understand what power the words "Grace" and "Mercy" represent? Do you know the true definition of these words? Grace means we are given what we don't deserve. Mercy suggests we are spared what we deserve. Both of these refer to God's favor toward us—favor we don't have to earn. God loves us so much He gives us these two powerful gifts on a daily basis. Many times we forget to acknowledge His help. We pass it off as "luck." Nothing is simply by chance or worldly nature if we believe in God's grace. Each time you have been relieved of a negative circumstance in your life, it is because God has given you His Grace and Mercy. He is always there, freely giving, as long as we don't begin putting road blocks in His way. We are the key to unlocking ALL of what God has to offer us. All we have to do is open our hearts, ask God to take control and trust Him to lead us forward.

"Make every effort to live in peace with all men and to be holy; without holiness no one will see the Lord. See to it that no one misses the Grace of God and that no bitter root grows up to cause trouble and defile many"—HEBREWS 12:14-15.

"As you know, we consider blessed those that have persevered. You have heard of Job's perseverance and have seen what the Lord finally brought about. The Lord is full of compassion and mercy"
—JAMES 5:11.

_____ *Your Thoughts*

Day 73

There will always be times when we look back and say "what if?" This is a human tendency we all have. We question our actions or the fact that we did not take action. What if I had done this or that? What if I had said more or said less? What if? As we reflect back on life, we must understand the truth. God is God and we are not. We cannot control what happens to another human being. We cannot control situations we will face in life. We can only control our own actions by the choices we make and the path on which we choose to walk. This does not mean we control our life as if we were masterminds. This means we can control our reactions to what we face in life. This means we should seek God in prayer and then trust Jesus to help us prepare for what happens. We have been given the Word of God as the truth and living water by which to live. As we press through those times of life when we hear ourselves asking the 'what if' questions, remember God's promises in His Word. Trust in God's plan, live according to the Word, and you will be blessed.

"For the Lord God is a sun and shield; the Lord bestows favor and honor; no good thing does He withhold from those whose walk is blameless. O Lord Almighty, blessed is the man who trusts in you"
—PSALM 84:11-12.

"Do not merely listen to the Word, and so deceive yourselves. Do what it says. Anyone who listens to the Word but does not do what it says is like a man who looks at his face in a mirror and after looking at himself, goes away and immediately forgets what he looks like. But the man who looks intently into the perfect law that gives freedom, and continues to do this, not forgetting what he has heard, but doing it – he will be blessed in what he does"— JAMES 1:22-25.

_____ *Your Thoughts*

Day 74

Are you at a point in your life where you feel isolated and alone? Do you feel as if no one understands or cares? Are you becoming somewhat resentful or bitter because your emotions are raging out of control? All of us have been there. Whether you're going through the fire right now or have been through it in the past, it is a very difficult place to be. Recognize that you are normal. You are not alone. Your battle can and will be overcome if you allow God to help. So often when we need God the most, we tend to shut Him out. It's when you don't feel like praying that you should pray more. It's when you don't feel like accepting help that you need help the most. It's when you feel like giving up that you should give it all to God. We cannot possibly press through the trials alone. The devil will use these difficult times to try and bring you down more. He will attempt to turn your attention away from the power of God. Keep in mind that this world has two spiritual realms—darkness and light. The light always, always overpowers the darkness. Jesus is the light. God gave us His only son Jesus to be our helper and our deliverer through each struggle. Allow Jesus to be your light—your source. God's amazing love, grace and mercy can and will carry you through. God's power is in your hands if you simply ask Him to show you the way. Don't expect instant results; instead, give God time to turn things around. Trusting in Him will give you power and peace to endure the challenge and to be an overcomer.

"When Jesus spoke again to the people, He said, 'I am the light of the world. Whoever follows me will never walk in darkness, but will have the light of life'"—JOHN 8:12.

"Do not be anxious about anything, but in everything, by prayer and petition, with thanksgiving, present your requests to God. And the peace of God, which transcends all understanding, will guard your hearts and your minds in Christ Jesus"—PHILIPPIANS 4:6-7.

_____ *Your Thoughts*

Day 75

Have you ever felt as if you didn't know how to take the next step forward? There are times in our lives when we face the unknown and we don't have a clue how to handle it. It may be a struggle that has left you feeling isolated or alone. It may be a new direction in life that has you terrified to step out of your comfort zone. You may be dealing with health issues that leave you scared and depleted. Whatever you are facing, you are not alone. All of us face things that require looking fear in the eyes. This is where faith steps in and gives us the ability to overcome these fears. God wants to give us the most this world has to offer. God desires to bless us abundantly. As we grow in our faith, we come to recognize how important it is to know these truths. When we seek God and trust that He has our best interests at heart, we can press past the fears. Jesus is our help and our comforter. Pray for God to give you wisdom and guidance. Ask Jesus to be your navigator and have confidence that you will not be alone. As we look at what today has to offer, know that God is with you, and as you walk forward, your steps will be guided through faith.

"I will instruct you and teach you in the way you should go; I will counsel you and watch over you"—PSALM 32:8.

"I can do everything through Him who gives me strength"
—PHILIPPIANS 4:13.

"You, dear children, are from God and have overcome them, because the One who is in you is greater than the one who is in the world"
—1 JOHN 4:4.

_____ *Your Thoughts*

Day 76 _____

Have you ever wanted to throw your hands up and yell, "Do over!" Sometimes we feel like hitting the delete button on sections of our lives. However, those times in which we wish we could ask for a "do over," are actually times of growth and wisdom. Yes, they may have been serious mistakes and wrong choices but God's amazing Grace takes over and those mistakes and choices can be turned around and forgiven. We must never forget that because of Jesus we have the opportunity to ask for a new beginning. Our lives are full of difficulties and trials. We will all make mistakes. These mistakes are not permanent and recognizing them and learning from them gives us wisdom. As we realize the times we have made choices that were not the best...let us determine to draw closer to God than ever. Dig into your faith, and simply talk to God about your desire to be forgiven. Prayer is our ability to take our sins to the cross. Ask Jesus to help you overcome the things you are struggling with. His love endures forever and His forgiving arms are awaiting you.

"For He has rescued us from the dominion of darkness and brought us into the kingdom of the Son He loves, in whom we have redemption, the forgiveness of sins"—COLOSSIANS 1:13-14.

"Praise be to the God and Father of our Lord Jesus Christ! In His great mercy He has given us new birth into a living hope through the resurrection of Jesus Christ from the dead, and into an inheritance that can never perish, spoil or fade – kept in heaven for you, who through faith are shielded by God's power until the coming of the salvation that is ready to be revealed in the last time. In this you greatly rejoice, though now for a little while you may have had to suffer grief in all kinds of trials. These have come so that your faith – of greater worth than gold, which perishes even though refined by fire – may be proved genuine and may result in praise, glory and honor when Jesus Christ is revealed"—1 PETER 1:3-9.

_____*Your Thoughts*

_____

_____

_____

_____

_____

_____

_____

_____

_____

_____

_____

_____

_____

_____

Day 77

I quit. I can't do this anymore. I don't understand why? I'm tired of trying. Do these phrases sound familiar? If you haven't .experienced this at some point in your life, you will. We all come to the end of our rope at one time or another. It's a heavy, lonely, hard place to be. At the time, it seems as if there is no answer...no way out of the situation...and no hope. As we reflect on those times in our lives, we can still experience the emotions. Isn't it awesome that you made it through? God was with you even when you felt alone. If you're experiencing this difficult time in your life right now know that God is there. It's during those trying times in our lives that we develop a closer relationship to our Creator. The times in which we suffer are when we are being refined and made stronger. Our suffering allows us the opportunity to seek Jesus and trust solely in God. Suffering prepares us to be empathetic. Every fire you have walked through...every obstacle you have overcome...has now become a testimony. We are the example of Christ in this world. We are the light in the midst of the darkness. Use your experiences to help others. Don't be afraid to share your journey for you can be assured that you will help someone who is walking in that valley right now. Rise up and know that God is with us.

"Therefore, since we have been justified through faith, we have peace with God through our Lord Jesus Christ, through whom we have gained access by faith into this grace in which we now stand. And we rejoice in the hope of the glory of God. Not only so, but we also rejoice in our sufferings, because we know that suffering produces perseverance, perseverance, character; and character, hope. And hope does not disappoint us, because God has poured out His love into our hearts by the Holy Spirit, whom He has given us"
—ROMANS 5:1-5.

"Therefore encourage one another and build each other up, just as in fact you are doing"—1 THESSALONIANS 5:11.

_____ *Your Thoughts*

Day 78

Life is full of difficult times. It's part of the human existence. Do you ever feel as if some people experience more difficulties than others? It's safe to say that most of us have had that thought when we're walking through the trials of life. We may look around and think that all the people surrounding us are filled with happiness and peace. The truth is we all deal with something every single day. Everyone faces different levels of trials at different times in our lives. As we face these times, we can do one of two things. We can pile the burdens upon our shoulders, and carry the weight of their existence around like baggage; or we can choose to seek Jesus to help us carry it all. Believing in Jesus does not exempt us from facing trials in our lives. Faith in God gives us power and the ability to have hope so we can walk through the tough stuff. It isn't easy to walk through life's valleys; however, it's comforting to know that no matter what, God is there and Jesus will help us endure.

"Have mercy on me, O God, have mercy on me, for in you my soul takes refuge. I will take refuge in the shadow of your wings until the disaster has passed. I cry out to God Most High, to God, who fulfills His purpose for me. He sends from Heaven and saves me, rebuking those who hotly pursue me; God sends His love and His faithfulness"—PSALM 57:1-3.

"Jesus said: 'Peace I leave with you; my peace I give you. I do not give to you as the world gives. Do not let your hearts be troubled and do not be afraid'"—JOHN 14:27.

_____ *Your Thoughts*

Day 79 _____

Some days it's difficult to wake up. It may not be because you're physically tired; you may simply be emotionally exhausted. Many times we're facing situations in our lives that we don't know how to handle. We would rather stay in bed, call into work, or hide from the world rather than face the difficulty we perceive in that day. Is it possible that the difficulty you are anticipating is much less than you perceive? Are you anxious, creating scenarios in your own mind and making the situation out to be much more than it really is? God's Word tells us, "We can do everything through Christ who strengthens us." (PHILIPPIANS 4:13) We know that God's promises are real; therefore, we must grab hold of His truth, knowing we can face anything in life with Christ. As humans, we tend to focus on what we see right in front of us. We fixate on the here and now, rather than on the hope we have in Christ. No matter how difficult things are in the present, there is healing and the ability to press through it. We must focus on the cross, seek Jesus on a continuous basis and pray to God, honestly and sincerely. Do not lose heart. Our troubles are momentary but hope is eternal.

"Therefore we do not lose heart. Though outwardly we are wasting away, yet inwardly we are being renewed day by day. For our light and momentary troubles are achieving for us an eternal glory that far outweighs them all. So we fix our eyes not on what is seen, but on what is unseen. For what is seen is temporary, but what is unseen is eternal"—2 CORINTHIANS 4:16-18.

"For we do not have a high priest who is unable to sympathize with our weaknesses, but we have one who has been tempted in every way, just as we are – yet was without sin. Let us then approach the throne of grace with confidence, so that we may receive mercy and find grace to help us in our time of need"—HEBREWS 4:15-16.

_____ *Your Thoughts*

Day 80

When it rains, it pours. How often have you heard that phrase before? Many times we experience cycles in our lives where we're faced with several difficult circumstances in a row. It feels like you're in a constant storm with the rain pouring down harder and harder with each incident. It's at these times when we might feel forgotten. You may have been trying and trying to fix and make sense of each situation, only to be bombarded with another situation, instead of finding answers or relief. You feel forgotten by God. We might begin asking God, "Where are you?" Or, "Why aren't you helping me?" This is when we feel weakest. Many times, we don't even know how or what to pray. The most powerful thing we can do during these times is to simply whisper the name of Jesus and call on the name of God. "Jesus, help me." "Jesus, show me what to do; God, I cannot do this without you." Surrendering has more power than anything our human flesh can attempt to fix things. We must trust that God is with us even when we don't understand. The power of prayer is effective and allows God to take over and the Holy Spirit to help us in our weakness. Believe that God is with you, and allow Jesus to carry you through. One day you will look back and be amazed at what you have overcome.

"Trust in the Lord with all your heart and lean not on your own understanding; in all your ways acknowledge Him, and He shall direct your path"—PROVERBS 3:5-6.

"But if we hope for what we do not yet have, we wait for it patiently. In the same way, the Spirit helps us in our weakness. We do not know what we ought to pray for, but the Spirit Himself intercedes for us with groans that words cannot express"—ROMANS 8:25-26.

_____ *Your Thoughts*

Day 81

When you have overcome an obstacle; when you've made a significant change for the better; when you have defeated the enemy; when you have asked God to forgive you, you have become a new creation. NEVER let the past...the mistakes...the hardships...or the hurts, drag you down. FOCUS on the outcome of today. ONLY look back to recognize the miracle that God has shown you through the things you have accomplished today. When you dwell in the past, you are allowing the enemy to remain in control, which hinders what God is trying to do for you. Embrace the success of your journey and give thanks to God who has, who does, and who will continue to line things up for an amazing future. Trust in Jesus to guide you and help you toward that future. Take pride in yourself for you are an amazing person who is worthy and valuable in every way!

"Therefore, if anyone is in Christ, he is a new creation; the old has gone, the new has come!"—2 CORINTHIANS 5:17.

"You used to walk in these ways, in the life you once lived. But now you must rid yourselves of all such things as these: anger, rage, malice, slander, and filthy language from your lips. Do not lie to each other, since you have taken off your old self with its practices and have put on the new self, which is being renewed in knowledge in the image of its Creator. Here there is no Greek or Jew, circumcised or uncircumcised, barbarian, Scythian, slave or free, but Christ is all, and is in all"—COLOSSIANS 3:7-11.

_____ *Your Thoughts*

Day 82

Why is it so hard to be honest about what we are going through in our lives? For the most part, people do as much as they can to hide the truth. Trying to hide from society, we attempt to put on our masks each day. We may be asked several times throughout the day, "How are you doing?" However, we never reply with the truth. Most of the time we respond with answers like, "Just fine," or "Good, how are you?" How often do we stop to listen to another person, to find out what's really going on in their lives? We hide our struggles, making every attempt to look our best. I believe the majority of the world takes on this false identity. If we're really honest about life, most of us are dealing with an inner struggle each day. Everyone goes through something difficult at some point in their lives. These times are when we feel alone and isolated. Praise God for the light we are able to see flickering in the distance. This light is the hope we have in Jesus. The most difficult times in our lives, are times of growth and maturity. During these times we must dig deeper into the Word of God and open our hearts to the love of God. God places people and situations in our paths to help us. These are the glimpses of light we need in order to press through. This is why it is so important to share our experiences and do all we can to be honest about our afflictions. The more we open up about our testimony, the more we are able to be that light for someone who is going through similar circumstances. Allow your light to shine for Jesus so you may help someone see the hope that lies ahead for them.

"But those who hope in the Lord will renew their strength. They will soar on wings like eagles; they will run and not grow weary, they will walk and not be faint"—ISAIAH 40:31.

"Jesus said: 'You are the light of the world. A city on a hill cannot be hidden. Neither do people light a lamp and put it under a bowl. Instead they put it on its stand, and it gives light to everyone in the house. In the same way, let your light shine before men, that they may see your good deeds and praise your Father in Heaven"
—MATTHEW 5:14-16.

_____ *Your Thoughts*

_____

_____

_____

_____

_____

_____

_____

_____

_____

_____

_____

_____

_____

_____

_____

Day 83_____

Are you listening? Can you hear it? Why can't we hear it?
Why isn't God talking to me? Why am I not getting answers to
my prayers and questions? We aren't listening. The human
mind is geared toward signal and response. Naturally we send
out our 'signals'...our prayers to God...and expect to hear an
instant response. Our reaction to the lack of response is
impatience and frustration. Typically, our next reaction to a lack
of response is to attempt to take an action of our own. This is
called "trying to be in control." You have heard it again and
again. Let go and let God. We get in the way of hearing what
God might be trying to tell us or show us...because we jump to
action before listening. Listening is a discipline that goes
against the nature of humans. Most of the time it's not a
'booming' vocal voice we hear. God speaks to us in subtle
ways...through nudging of the Holy Spirit...or sometimes
through other people. When we impatiently expect immediate
answers...we lose the capability of hearing from God. Slow
down and listen. Spend time in prayer and relationship with
God...and you will begin to hear God's direction.

*"Let the wise listen and add to their learning, and let the discerning
get guidance"—PROVERBS 1:5.*

*"Then you will call upon me and come and pray to me, and I will
listen to you. You will seek me and find me when you seek me with all
your heart"—JEREMIAH 29:12-13.*

*"But do not forget this one thing my friends: With the Lord a day is
like a thousand years, and a thousand years are like a day. The Lord
is not slow in keeping his promise, as some understand slowness. He is
patient with you, not wanting anyone to perish, but everyone to come
to repentance"—2 PETER 3:8-9.*

_Your Thoughts

Day 84

Sometimes there seems to be no answer. It's a very difficult place to be. We face hardships in life and find ourselves barely hanging on. We battle to figure out the why's and how's of the situation. We talk to God and plead for His direction. The silence is deafening. Why do we have to go through these empty dry periods of our life? Why don't we feel like we're being heard? Why do we feel as if our prayers are mere words and there seems to be no answer? Why? Because we are human and we're not able to foresee what God is working on. God is everything. God is everywhere. God is here, now, and forever. God does not go away...we do. When we're faced with hardship and difficult times in our lives, we feel weak. We begin to doubt and then we start thinking too much. When we don't see instant results and solutions to the issues, we attempt to take control. Yes, we may pray and pray and pray but how many of those prayers are total surrender? When you find yourself at this difficult place in life, it's time to put up a fight. Pick up your Bible and begin to seek. Read the Scriptures. Then, kneel to the floor and whole heartedly talk to God. Ask Jesus to take over and hold your Hand. When you stand back up, reach your hands out and say, "I walk with you, Jesus." Life is not always going to be easy but it will always be possible with God in control. You may not be able to understand things in the moment but if you will trust in God there will be a moment when you can look back and say, "I made it through."

"When Jesus spoke again to the people, He said: 'I am the light of the world. Whoever follows me will never walk in darkness, but will have the light of life'"—JOHN 8:12.

"Do not be anxious about anything, but in everything, by prayer and petition, with thanksgiving, present your requests to God. And the peace of God, which transcends all understanding, will guard your hearts and your minds in Christ Jesus"—PHILIPPIANS 4:6-7.

_____*Your Thoughts*

Day 85 _____

Are you suffering with painful, chronic or terminal medical issues right now? Is your heart heavy because you've experienced the death of a loved one? Are you in financial debt, jobless or wondering how you're going to make ends meet? Are you lost, uncertain about the next step to take? Has someone hurt you, physically or emotionally? Have you been so extremely violated that you don't know if you'll ever overcome it? Are you facing divorce, addiction, depression, eating disorders or other huge mountains that seem impossible to climb? Every one of us faces something each day. You may not be faced with major trials today, but at some point in life you either have or you will. This is called life; however, there is a way up and over every single barrier you may face. His name is Jesus. We have the opportunity to make one of two choices. We can either fall down or we can ask Jesus to help pick us up. Jesus suffered more than any human mind can comprehend. He endured it all and willingly died, shedding His blood so we could have the opportunity to be saved. Jesus was resurrected from death to bring us salvation and hope. We have a choice today because of His suffering. If you feel as if there is no hope, no purpose, no direction and no way out of the pit you are in, then look at your palm. Somewhere, in the lines running across your palm, you will find an image of the cross—two lines, intersecting with each other. The cross represents love...hope...and eternal life. Ask Jesus to help you. Allow God to show you how to handle things. Never give up. He never gives up on us. He wants us to ask for help.

"Cast your cares on the Lord and He will sustain you; He will never let the righteous fall"—PSALM 55:22.

"But if we hope for what we do not yet have, we wait for it patiently"
—ROMANS 8:25

Your Thoughts

Day 86 _____

When you are facing something difficult, do you ever find yourself asking the same question over and over? This could be a 'why' question or a 'how' question. The most common questions I hear, are "Why are these things happening to me?" and "How can I get through this?" We face times in our lives where we just don't know. We don't know the 'why' and we sure don't know the 'how'. What we must remember is we are not alone. God is with us. Not only is God with us, He places people in our lives to help us press through these difficult times. Many times we're so overwhelmed and frustrated with our difficulties that we don't recognize the presence of God. We may be angry at God. We may feel abandoned. The truth is we are the ones who block God out. Our human minds want solutions and answers. When we cannot get results or answers to what we are facing, we become defensive and attempt to be in control. This is human nature and something we all go through. God understands. God sent His Son Jesus into this world for us. Jesus lived as we live. He faced difficulties as we do. He questioned as we question. Jesus understands our emotions. As we press through the valleys of life, let us seek the arms of Jesus. Be comforted in knowing you can be honest about your emotions and openly speak to God about how you are feeling. God will carry you through each trial, and Jesus is always available to hold your hand.

"So do not fear, for I am with you; do not be dismayed, for I am your God. I will strengthen you and help you; I will uphold you with my righteous right hand"—ISAIAH 41:10.

"The Lord is good, a refuge in times of trouble. He cares for those who trust in Him"—NAHUM 1:7.

"Blessed is the man who perseveres under trial, because when he has stood the test, he will receive the crown of life that God has promised to those who love Him"—JAMES 1:12.

_____ *Your Thoughts*

Day 87

Cancer, death, divorce, disease, debt and all the other major issues we face in our lives can be debilitating. Everyone knows someone going through something major. This is the truth of life as we know it. As we face these major obstacles, we find ourselves going through a roller coaster of emotions. At the onset of a major issue, most people receive an abundant amount of support and compassion from others. Often, we have family or friends that step in and help and doing the best they know how. But after a certain amount of time, life moves on and the people who were initially there move on as well. Those facing the major issues find themselves suddenly alone. It's the weeks and months following the major obstacle in life that can become a time of vulnerability. Faith becomes a struggle, doubt sets in and the devil begins attacking. This is when people who are struggling need help the most. I've often heard the excuse that people don't know what to say to someone who is struggling. We don't need to know exactly what to say but we can allow God to work through us. As Christians, we are called to help others. We are asked to be encouragers and to help strengthen the weak. It's essential for everyone to pay attention to those who are struggling. Call them. Pray with them. Bring them hope through showing you care and letting them know you haven't forgotten them. It takes a few extra minutes of your day to make a major difference in someone's life. Help those who are struggling to see that God is with them. It's through the love of others that people will begin to see the hope in Jesus.

"Finally, all of you, live in harmony with one another; be sympathetic, love as brothers, be compassionate and humble"—1 PETER 3:8.

"And we urge you, brothers, warn those who are idle, encourage the timid, help the weak, be patient with everyone"
—1THESSALONIANS 5:14.

"May the God of hope fill you with all joy and peace as you trust in Him, so that you may overflow with hope by the power of the Holy Spirit"—ROMANS 15:13.

_____ *Your Thoughts*

_____

_____

_____

_____

_____

_____

_____

_____

_____

_____

_____

_____

_____

_____

Day 88

Why me? How can this be happening? What am I doing wrong? These are questions we've all faced at some point in our lives. When we face adversity, we begin searching for a reason why. It's the human response to wonder why our Creator, our Father in Heaven would allow these difficult things to happen. It makes no sense to us. We want to fix things and we begin to analyze the situation trying figure out why it happened in the first place. How many of us have gone through this cycle repeatedly in our lives? Since the beginning of creation, humans have struggled with this cycle of faith. Faith is not easy. Faith is something we develop. Faith is hope. Hope is what we must hold onto in order to press through the difficult times and understand these times are temporary. We cannot possibly understand the depths of those things that happen to us. The one thing we can control is our reaction to these trials. It's the reaction and then action we take that will determine our inner peace. The situation may not change immediately, but if we learn to seek God and open our heart to trust Jesus, we can begin a new walk of faith. The more we allow ourselves to understand that God is the One who will help us, the more we grow in strength. God is who has the ultimate power and control. Jesus will help. God is really there. We just need to break down our walls and truly let God in.

"Trust in the Lord with all your heart and lean not on your own understanding. In all your ways acknowledge Him, and He shall direct your path"—PROVERBS 3:5-6.

"Now faith is being sure of what we hope for and certain of what we do not see"—HEBREWS 11:1.

"Dear friends, do not be surprised at the painful trial you are suffering, as though something strange were happening to you. But rejoice that you participate in the sufferings of Christ, so that you may be overjoyed when His glory is revealed. If you are insulted because of the name of Christ, you are blessed, for the Spirit of glory and of God rests on you"—1 PETER 4:12-14.

_Your Thoughts

Day 89

Life is full of memories. Some memories make us smile while others make us cringe with internal pain. Either way, the things we remember are what have brought us to where we are today. It's important to remind ourselves to reflect on our life journey with the determination to find the positive, even in the midst of the pain. Not long ago, I faced the responsibility of going through my daughter's belonging for the first time since her passing. Just a few days after she died, we were forced to move her entire apartment contents into a storage unit. As I faced opening that storage unit, I asked God to prepare my heart for the emotional task. There are no words to describe the feelings one goes through when faced with seeing the physical memories of a loved one who has gone on to Heaven. Jesus carried me through that day and He carries each one of us through every difficult thing we must face. The difficulties we go through mold us and refine us on a continual basis. We develop strength, integrity and wisdom when we have walked through life's trials. As I reflected on memories with my Ashley, I found the joy and the comfort of knowing she is with our Heavenly Father. I have peace and a positive outlook, knowing I can trust in God's promises. As we reflect on our past, we see evidence of God's presence. We have all climbed mountains and sunk into valleys, but we also have victory in Jesus. Our life journey is not easy but there is always hope in God.

"Jesus said: 'Peace I leave with you; my peace I give you. I do not give to you as the world gives. Do not let your hearts be troubled and do not be afraid'"—JOHN 14:27.

"But thanks be to God! He gives us the victory through our Lord Jesus Christ. Therefore, my dear brothers, stand firm. Let nothing move you. Always give yourselves fully to the work of the Lord, because you know that your labor in the Lord is not in vain"
—1 CORINTHIANS 15:57-58.

_____ *Your Thoughts*

Day 90

What are we waiting for? This question is endless. Each day is a waiting game. We wait for things all day long. Our days may begin with the subconscious wait for our alarms to awaken us. We may wait for coffee to brew, traffic lights to change, people to show up, meetings to begin or end, doctors' appointments, food to arrive, or the sun to set so we can await the time to go to bed. We all wait for something. For the most part, life ticks along one day at a time. But what if you're waiting for something much grander and much more life-changing? What if you're waiting for medical results? What if you're waiting for a loved one to return home from military deployment? What if you're waiting on the birth of a precious baby? Sometimes we're praying for miracles to happen, waiting for God to show us signs of His presence. Each step we take in life has an element of trust within it. We must trust that God is with us and that HE will guide us through all these moments of waiting. As we seek Jesus to help us each day, we must remember that not all things are going to turn out as we always want. There will be times when things don't make sense and you're left waiting for more answers. The key is prayer and patience. Be still. God is sovereign. Hope is real. Have faith that one day you will understand and trust that Jesus is with you.

"I waited patiently for the Lord; He turned to me and heard my cry. He lifted me out of the slimy pit, out of the mud and mire; He set my feet on a rock and gave me a firm place to stand"—PSALM 40:1-2.

"Yet the Lord longs to be gracious to you; He rises to show you compassion. For the Lord is a God of justice. Blessed are all who wait for Him"—ISAIAH 30:18.

"But if we hope for what we do not yet have, we wait for it patiently"—ROMANS 8:25.

_____ *Your Thoughts*

_____

_____

_____

_____

_____

_____

_____

_____

_____

_____

_____

_____

_____

_____

_____

About the author

Layla Freeman is a wife, mother, friend and encourager to all. She is the author of the weekday encouragement devotional blog, *Layla's Light*, which she has been writing since 2001. Layla's blog can be found on Facebook, Twitter and at www.laylafreeman.com.

Layla is also a Business Owner/Vice President, a Stephen Ministry Leader, Lay Servant/Speaker, Congregational Care Minister and volunteer for several worthy community causes.

She is also the C.E.O. and Founder of the Non-Profit ministry, "Light of Hope, Inc." This ministry outreach was created to help individuals and families who are struggling with addiction, depression and other life difficulties.

Because of her personal experiences during extreme difficulties in life, Layla has a passion to help others who are facing trials. Her writing is empowered by the truth of God's unconditional love and forgiveness and the hope we find in God's promises.

A portion of this book's proceeds will go directly to the Non-Profit outreach, "Light of Hope, Inc." If you wish to make a tax-deductible donation, please send it to P.O. Box 669, Claremore, OK 74018.

For more information about this ministry, please check out the website at *www.lightofhopeinc.org*.

Praise for Layla's Light

I began reading "Layla's Light" a few years back. Through replying to her daily messages, we began to keep in contact via messenger. Ironically, Layla and I had very similar pasts, even though we live thousands of miles apart. I learned through Layla's light, how to deal with life in all its adversities in a more positive way, by letting go of resentments of the past that held me back for years. I also learned that God could and would be there for me. Once I began to put my total trust in him, my fear and anxiety began bit by bit to lift. I suddenly felt this inner peace that I had never felt before, by letting go and handing my will and life over to him. I firmly believe that the Lord works through people and they are sent to you for a reason. I have no doubt that Layla was sent to me to give me the knowledge of how God works in your life when you seek him. Without God, we are nothing. By reading "Layla's light" on a daily basis, my life has changed so much for the better. I now can face whatever life throws at me, knowing God is with me all the way. Layla has been a total inspiration to me and opened my eyes to a new way of living. I thank the Lord for sending her. She saved my life from being full of fear, depression and dread, to having peace of mind, serenity and abundance. Thank you my friend.

Colette Doherty
Eire, Ireland

God lead me to "Layla's Light" during a time of great sorrow. My daughter was struggling with the world, abandoning her Christian faith. I was put into a situation in which I had no control. "Layla's Light" started coming into my Facebook feed and the readings were like God speaking directly to me. I noticed Layla had a P.O. Box in Claremore, Oklahoma, the exact place my daughter had just moved! When visiting at Christmastime, I messaged Layla, asking for her church address. The church just so happened to be located across the street from where my daughter was living! I pulled into the parking lot with tears in my eyes, overwhelmed with God's presence. In awe of how much He loves us, I was just praising Him and thanking Him for this confirmation that He is with me.

On Christmas Eve 2015, I had a God ordained meeting with the author of "Layla's Light," Layla Freeman. It was such an honor, and like we had been lifelong friends. Seeds were planted in my daughter that I trust God will water, grow and mature into something beautiful. Beauty from ashes! In Jesus' name!

Andrea Flaherty
San Diego, CA

Layla and I met approximately a year and a half ago on Facebook, on a post called Layla's Light. As I continued to read her daily posts, I felt as if the Lord was using her as a vessel to me from You, Lord. For you see, I have been bedridden for approximately three years. I never left the house except to go to doctors, and then it was right back home. So, I was very alone. I would lay in my bed thinking, "What good am I to You, Lord?" Layla was so encouraging, telling me how important I was and just how many people I was reaching and helping. She actually called me a Prayer Warrior. I had never thought of myself as anything of any importance. Thank you, Layla, for that. As I continued to read her daily posts, I also started reading some of her other friends' comments. As the Lord led me to them, I would ask if I could pray for them. I would pray for them and then asked if they needed friendship. They were more than welcome, because I would accept their friendship. It has been a two-way street, because I'm being blessed for helping other people and I feel blessed that the Lord allows me to do His will. It wasn't too long after this, that one day Layla ask if I wanted to become a personal friend with her. She is a remarkable woman of God. The things in life she has gone through—the ups and downs—she has overcome with victory through the Lord. She's not afraid to share her trials because she's experienced a lot of things others have. My life has totally changed and now I'm up out-of-bed. I actually went on my first little vacation in three years. The Lord is working miracles in my life, bringing healing and restoration just as He promised! God will get all the glory for my healing.
Layla, I love you dearly for you're my little angel and my sister-in-Christ. Be blessed and know our Lord is with us always.

Nancy Kelly
San Bernadino, California

Made in the
USA
Lexington, KY